Public Expenditure and Income Distribution in Malaysia

This book studies the impact of public expenditure allocations in achieving income equality goals in Malaysia.

The book examines the initial functional and institutional distribution of income across different institutional agents and sectors and evaluates the impact of the public expenditure policies in reducing the inter-ethnic and rural–urban disparity. Since Malaysia has made enormous progress in eliminating poverty, the authors suggest that a change of emphasis in the public expenditure policy may now be called for. They present evidence on the importance of public expenditure in improving income inequality and examine the initial functional and institutional distribution of income across different institutional agents and sectors. The development of the Social Accounting Matrix (SAM) model that presents both economic and social statistics in an economy can be served as a useful tool of this work. The SAM model is used to evaluate the impact of the public expenditure policies in reducing inter-ethnic and rural–urban disparity.

A comprehensive source of information on how to deal with inequality economic challenges, the book will be of interest to economists and researchers on Southeast Asian Studies.

Mukaramah Harun is Professor at the School of Economics, Finance and Banking, Universiti Utara Malaysia.

Sze Ying Loo received her PhD degree from the School of Economics, Finance and Banking, Universiti Utara Malaysia.

Routledge Contemporary Southeast Asia Series

The aim of this series is to publish original, high-quality work by both new and established scholars on all aspects of Southeast Asia.

For more information about this series, please visit: www.routledge.com/ Routledge-Contemporary-Southeast-Asia-Series/book-series/RCSEA

Public Expenditure and Income Distribution in Malaysia

Mukaramah Harun
and Sze Ying Loo

Routledge
Taylor & Francis Group

LONDON AND NEW YORK

First published 2023
by Routledge
4 Park Square, Milton Park, Abingdon, Oxon OX14 4RN

and by Routledge
605 Third Avenue, New York, NY 10158

Routledge is an imprint of the Taylor & Francis Group, an informa business

© 2023 Mukaramah Harun and Sze Ying Loo

British Library Cataloguing-in-Publication Data
A catalogue record for this book is available from the British Library

Library of Congress Cataloging-in-Publication Data
Names: Mukaramah Harun, author. | Loo, Sze Ying, author.
Title: Public expenditure and income distribution in Malaysia / Mukaramah Harun, Sze Ying Loo.
Description: Abingdon, Oxon ; New York, NY : Routledge, 2023. | Series: Routledge contemporary Southeast Asia series | Includes bibliographical references and index.
Identifiers: LCCN 2022015246 (print) | LCCN 2022015247 (ebook) | ISBN 9781032298849 (hardback) | ISBN 9781032298863 (paperback) | ISBN 9781003302506 (ebook)
Subjects: LCSH: Income distribution—Malaysia. | Government spending policy—Malaysia. | Structural adjustment (Economic policy)—Malaysia. | Social accounting—Malaysia. | Malaysia—Appropriations and expenditures. | Malaysia—Economic policy.
Classification: LCC HC445.5.Z9 M85 2023 (print) | LCC HC445.5.Z9 (ebook) | DDC 339.3595—dc23/eng/20220509
LC record available at https://lccn.loc.gov/2022015246
LC ebook record available at https://lccn.loc.gov/2022015247

ISBN: 978-1-032-29884-9 (hbk)
ISBN: 978-1-032-29886-3 (pbk)
ISBN: 978-1-003-30250-6 (ebk)

DOI: 10.4324/9781003302506

Typeset in Baskerville
by Apex CoVantage, LLC

Contents

Preface

High economic growth and wealth creation are always the focus of both political attention and public policy worldwide. However, the life quality of a country's population is now becoming increasingly important for the equality agenda. Since the equivalence of high economic growth and social well-being, especially the desire for equality of income is always in question, here comes the influential role that the governments play in the economy to sustain economic growth and well-being. A great amount of attention is then paid to public expenditure that is considered the most important economic tool the government has for managing allocation of resources directly in the desired area, and, most importantly, to infuse income distribution.

Malaysia has made remarkable achievements in handling economic hardships without ignoring the people's quality of life. Strikingly, high-priority-related programs were always high on the list of expenditure to ensure high efficiency in income distribution. Since the emergence of the concept of eradicating poverty and restructuring society in the national policies, the overall incidence of poverty has constantly been falling over the decades, while the country's economy was able to recover swiftly from the worst economic downturns in global markets. At the same time, the country saw very low rates of inflation and high growth in employment. Nonetheless, the unbalanced distribution of wealth between the different ethnic groups has still been the case and there is room for improvement for the income equality goals. The urban–rural income gap remains high where the urban population has remarkably higher incomes than the rural population. Moreover, the income share of the rich makes up a major portion of the country's total income where the gap between the share of the rich (the income levels of the top 20 percent) and the poor (the income levels of the bottom 40 percent) is wide. It would undermine economic performance and cause social tensions.

Typically, public expenditure is used as a primary tool to restructure the economy to achieve income equality goals. This motive matters as the most the fundamental pattern of public expenditure allocations. This book is primarily concerned with the impact of public expenditure allocations in achieving income equality goals in Malaysia. The emphasis is very much on the effect of public expenditure expansion by total and by different divisions on income distribution through various ethnic groups across regions (rural–urban) that are clearly reflected in the chapters. This book is intended for providing a comprehensive source of information that is detailed enough to give a clear and functional direction, especially in dealing with the inequality economic challenge that is not limited to Malaysia.

Figures and Tables

Figures

Tables

1 Introduction

1.1 General

The role of the government in economic growth and income distribution could be executed by its expenditure. The government can shape directly the income distribution through its expenditure design and pattern. Its primary concern is on the efforts toward ensuring government efficiency in income distribution that requires measures to increase high-priority-related programs and to reduce expenditure on low-priority-related programs. This is to ensure that the government expenditure for achieving the objective of income distribution policies is utilized efficiently. Usually, the government just simply states that the aim is to increase overall expenditure without specifying how. As a result, the government may distribute the expansions in any way it likes. Yet the income distribution impact will obviously be very different depending on whether it is an increase in the pay of civil servants, or an increase in the spending on health, or an increase in the spending in primary education in rural areas.

It is thus very enlightening to be able to see the impacts of government expenditure expansions on income distribution not only by the total expenditure but also by the class of expenditure. The effects are of two types: Upstream effects concern goods and factor services brought by the government sector. Should the government sector increase spending on road building, employment and employer/employee earnings, the private works sector would rise sharply, given the heavy weight of government contracts. The other effects are downstream. If schools are opened in rural areas, rural families will gain income that is equal to the service provided free of charge. Normally only this downstream effect is analyzed. For this reason, this book devises instruments capable of calculating all the upstream effects of an expansion in the public sector expenditure called the Social Accounting Matrix (SAM).

The issue of inequality is crucial because it has been shown in the literature that growth will lead to poverty reduction if inequality is addressed

DOI: 10.4324/9781003302506-1

at the same time, and if wealth is very unequally distributed, it may cause slower economic growth (Roberto, 1996; Persson & Tabellini, 1994; Alesine & Rodrik, 1992). In other words, growth, if it occurs, will not be sustainable if inequality is not addressed. More importantly, for Malaysia as a multi-ethnic country, if income inequality becomes serious, social conflicts may become intense and violence may begin to emerge.

Income inequality is still a crucial matter for Malaysia despite the favorable economic growth and huge public spending on economic development. Due to this, the government now emphasizes more on the issue of efficiency and effectiveness of the public sector expenditure to ensure that the core objective of the government policy of reducing poverty and income equality is achieved. In the Eleventh Malaysia Plan, a more effective government expenditure policy including the implementation and monitoring mechanism emphasizing outcomes and impacts is emphasized. All government agencies are required to ensure that their policies and programs take into account the implications on distribution. Close attention is given to the impact of programs and projects. Government expenditure will focus on projects and programs that will generate maximum multiplier effects, extensive geographical spillover as well as minimum leakages. These projects include human resource development as well as the provision of social and physical infrastructure, particularly in the rural areas to improve accessibility and further improve income disparities. This brings about the importance of the analysis on the impact of public expenditure expansion by total and by different categories on income distribution in Malaysia. This could probably answer the question whether the public expenditure is allocated through the appropriate programs to reach the poor, or in other words, whether the public sector is efficiently and effectively allocating its expenditure by considering the impact on the poor.

Generally, this book analyzes the impact of the public expenditure on income distribution in Malaysia. Specifically, the objectives of the book are to examine the initial functional and institutional distribution of income across different institutional agents and sectors and to evaluate the impact of the public expenditure policies in reducing the inter-ethnic and rural–urban disparity.

This book begins with an introduction of the public expenditure and income distribution concepts, and a review on the theoretical view of the government's role in economic developments, especially in income distributions. Chapter 2 presents some of the characteristic features of the Malaysian economy and the trend of poverty and income equality throughout the 1965 to 2010s period. The chapter also reviews the major policies that have been implemented to achieve the objective of poverty reduction and income equality. Chapter 3 starts with a general view on what is SAM, architecture of the Malaysian SAM and an overview of the SAM-based methodology for inference under fixed-price multiplier methods. Chapter 4 presents the results of the analysis and the interpretation of the results. Finally, Chapter 5 provides the conclusion and policy implications.

1.2 Public Expenditure and Income Distribution

The question of how the effects of public expenditure on income distribution are analyzed lies in the views of the differing theories of the government that will be presented later. One views the government as a neutral arbiter, mediated through the electoral process. In contrast, the radical perspective views the government as part and parcel of the capitalist economic and social system. With the transformation of competitive capitalism into monopoly capitalism, the role of the government will be more complex. In the absence of any offsetting tendencies, inequality becomes more severe over time in monopoly capitalism. For instance, in the acquisition of human capital, individuals starting in a family with more economic wealth and more human capital will tend to acquire relatively more human capital. Similarly, with physical capital, firms that start out with more physical capital and a larger share in the market have important economic advantages in market control, investment funds, information, and research and development to exacerbate the inequality over time. When inequality becomes more and more severe in each time period, the government must penetrate into society more and more to offset the socially destructive aspects of this inequality. The extent to which the government will mitigate the growing inequalities is conditioned by the need to perform its system maintenance function through its expenditure mechanism.

The government affects the distribution of income through the government purchasing policy, which affects companies, industries and workers differentially. Companies receive higher profits from government purchases than from non-government purchases, and consequently, stockholders in those industries, *ceteris paribus*, will receive higher dividends. These higher profits are derived from the nature of contracting with the government in which a high profit rate is guaranteed by the government. In addition, favorable relations with the government via contracting enable those industries to expand their plant capacity faster than would otherwise be the case.

The distributional impact of the government expenditure policy not only affects corporate profits and dividends, but the higher profit structure also places the company in a vulnerable bargaining position for labor to negotiate higher wage rates. Hence, it will affect the wage distribution (and thereby income distribution) as workers in some industries receive higher wages solely as a function of that government's purchasing relations. Therefore, the government expenditure policy influences wage structure via its influence over the structure of industries. Wages will be a positive function of the proportion of a sector's output purchased by the government after controlling the other forces affecting individual wage differences. The structure of a sector will be influenced by the purchasing policy of the government which will manifest itself in higher profits per worker.

It is important to recognize that the government influences the process by which people obtain income and thereby structures the income distribution. The government benefits certain groups in the society by purchasing goods and services from them rather than from other groups. An even more important distributive activity of the government is in defining and maintaining the institutional structure in which one group can benefit by owning enterprises which are sold to the government.

The impact of the government expenditure policy on wage structures can be viewed in the light of different characteristics of jobs and different characteristics of individuals. Typically, the urban manufacturing sector contains the privileged members of the labor force as there are relatively good working conditions, high pay, job security, promotion based on seniority and so on. This sector has evolved jobs with substantial skill specificity, acquired through formal education or on-the-job training. The agricultural sector, on the other hand, consists of jobs that do not possess much skill specificity. The labor pool to fill these jobs is comparatively undifferentiated, approaching a homogenous group. There is little or no on-the-job training required for performing these jobs. The labor is characterized by poor work discipline, high rates of turnover, unreliability on the job and the like. As a consequence, jobs in the agriculture sector pay low wages, have poor working conditions, provide little job security and have a high turnover.

With a view to understanding how the government expenditure serves as a central instrument in pursuit of the income distribution policy goals, it is useful to analytically classify the various components of the government expenditure in terms of their influence on various segments of the economy. The government expenditure typically is classified into current and capital expenditure. Current expenditure represents the consumption and capital expenditure represents assets creation by the government. Current expenditure, known as non-developmental expenditure, constitutes government administration expenditure, emoluments, supplies and services, pensions, interest payments, debt service charges and other non-productive services. Capital expenditure or also known as developmental expenditure constitutes government investment in the agricultural sector, trade and industry, transport, communication, technology, poverty alleviation, education, health, housing and employment generation.

With the classification of different classes of government expenditure, it is possible to identify the role of each of the various components of expenditure in the achievement of the equity goals through the operation of intermediate targets as schematized in Figure 1.1 below which is adapted from Pattnaik, Bose, Bhattacharyya, and Chander (2006). Typically, the fiscal policy sets growth, stability and equity as the ultimate goals where government expenditure management is one of the main operating instruments in pursuing these goals. In this pursuit, the government expenditure management plans to achieve intermediate targets set for overall expenditure control; balance budget, strategic resource allocation and strategic scale of expenditure by effective and responsive operational management of expenditure. The economic growth and equity goals are normally more responsive to development expenditure but the achievement of equity goals is more responsive to selective expenditure, particularly investment in poverty alleviation, education, health and employment generation. Slightly different from Pattnaik et al. (2006), this book views that current expenditure could also influence the equity goal, particularly emoluments. Some economists view that the government expenditure has to be balanced so as to pursue the goals of growth and equity while at the same time keeping a vigil on the overall size of the expenditure to contain the deficit within levels consistent with macroeconomic stability.

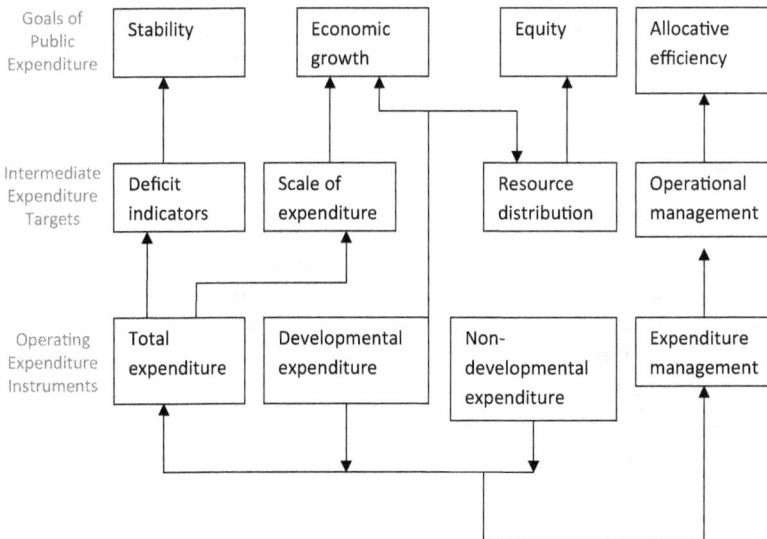

Figure 1.1 Fiscal Policy Operating Procedure and Government Expenditure

Source: Adapted from Pattnaik et al. (2006, p. 607)

1.3   The Concept of Income Distribution

Income distribution has always been a central concern of the economic theory as well as the economic policy. Classical economists such as Adam Smith, David Ricardo and Thomas Malthus were mainly concerned with factor income distribution; the distribution of income between the main factors of production, labor, capital and land. Modern economists have also addressed this issue, but have been more concerned with the distribution of income across individuals or households.

The concept of income inequality is distinct from poverty. Income distribution according to modern economists is the dispersion of incomes across an individual or households within a society. The appropriate level of income distribution analysis depends on why the information is needed. If the aim is to assess income and an individualistic approach to income is adopted, then the individual is the appropriate level. However, for some important aspects of income, the relevant distribution is among groups, not individuals, such as the distribution of income between different ethnic groups and regions.

On the other hand, poverty can be viewed in two ways – as a phenomenon of relative differences in income within a society, or in absolute terms, in relation to a defined poverty line. Oppenheim (1993) said that absolute poverty is when people fall below the level when they cannot house, clothe or feed themselves. Meanwhile relative poverty is when people are denied access to what is generally regarded as a reasonable standard and quality of life in that society. According to Rowntree (1901), the first rigorous definition of poverty identified poverty as an economic situation which rendered an individual or family unit incapable of maintaining a minimum acceptable living standard. This doctrine is based on the 'poverty line' based on the consumption levels required to survive.

Some economics scholars think that the income inequality accentuates poverty (Persson & Tabellini, 1994); others (Dollar & Kraay, 2002; Gustafsson & Johansson, 1999) believe that the relationship between income inequality and poverty is inverse. The inverse relationship between income inequality and poverty rate views a shift in income in favor of the rich is not necessarily at the expense of the poor.

Among the most common metrics used to measure inequality are the Gini index, the Theil index and the Hoover index. The Gini index measures the degree of inequality in the distribution of family income in a country. The index is calculated from the Lorenz curve, in which the cumulative family income is plotted against the number of families arranged from the poorest to the richest. The range of the Gini index is between 0 and 1 (0 percent and 100 percent) where 0 indicates perfect equality and 1 indicates maximum inequality.

1.4 Theoretical Views on the Government Involvement in Income Distribution

1.4.1 Kuznets' 'Inverted U Theory'

Early work on income distribution by Kuznets (1956) called the 'inverted U' theory hypothesizes that income inequality increases over time while a country is developing, and then after a certain average income is attained, inequality begins to decrease. The theory suggests that at a very low-income and low-average education, mainly in agricultural societies, income is more equally distributed because most workers have very low levels of education and are engaged in agriculture. Incomes are concentrated at low levels and concentration dominates the distribution of income. As the level of education rises, the distribution of income becomes more unequal, these societies become more urbanized and income distribution tends toward greater inequality. This is both because of differences between urban and rural incomes and because of greater income inequality within urban areas, where worker skills and payoff to skills tend to vary more than they do in rural areas. As average education in societies reaches very high levels, the distribution of education becomes more equal again and income distribution tends to become much more equal.

1.4.2 Competitive Market Theory

Traditionally, economists have shown little interest in the government's role in income distributional issues. The neo-classical view of economics lays on the attainment of the efficiency of resource allocation for any income distribution. If the government leaves economic actors alone, unfettered competitive markets would work better in promoting faster economic growth and generating socially desirable outcomes. The point of view holds that, except on rare occasions, the government should not intrude in markets and taxes should be low. The government spending should be restrained and, for the most part, government finances should be kept in balance, even at the cost of limiting social investment in government goods. Wages should not be supported by government regulations or social programs but eyed closely and disciplined if they rise fast because they are a source of inflation.

The Adam Smith theorem of the invisible hand states that if each consumer is allowed to choose freely what to buy and each producer is allowed to choose freely what to sell and how to produce it, the market will settle on a product distribution and prices that are beneficial to all the individual members of a community, and hence to the community as a whole. The reason for this is that self-interest drives actors to beneficial behavior.

effect of redistribution on the marginal propensity to consume out of income. Hence Keynes is unable to say whether one form of government expenditure is superior to another as long as both accomplish the macro objectives.

1.4.3   Theorem of Welfare Economics

The private sector, however, cannot be counted on to make investments in public goods that maximize economic and social returns. Economists acknowledge that private markets often fail to create adequate incentives to support government investments with high social returns. Thus, the government must be a participant in building an economy's productive capacity.

Economists often use the theory of market failure found in welfare economics as a rational for government activity. Market failures here refer to situations in which a voluntary transaction does not result in an efficient allocation such as the provision of public goods, externalities, imperfect information, monopoly and unemployment. Public goods such as infrastructure cannot be provided through the market system. Private investors may find the provision of infrastructure not profitable. In addition, as market economies have always been characterized by fluctuations in the business cycle, macroeconomic stabilization is something crucial. The government has to bear the responsibility of maintaining macroeconomic stability as the private sector has no incentive to make contributions to its realization.

Stiglitz (1991) in his working paper of "The Invisible Hand and Modern Welfare Economics", wrote that market interventions can make everyone better off in the matter of the limitations on information and risk distribution opportunities. The Invisible Hand often does not work in risk markets that are incomplete and information is too, imperfect. He therefore claimed that information imperfections are an important reason why the government should intervene in the market.

In this theorem of welfare economics, even if a competitive market might generate a Pareto-efficient allocation of resources, there are still cases for government intervention because an efficient allocation of resources might entail great inequality. For any Pareto-efficient allocation, there exists a set of prices that supports that allocation as market equilibrium, but each with a different distribution of welfare. The issue is to decide which Pareto-efficient allocation conforms to society's notion of distributive justice. Apparently, the market cannot do it. The social welfare function is obviously not a market construct; it must evolve from the government action process. Moreover, the Pareto principle can be pushed up further to allow economic efficiency to encompass not just actual Pareto improvement but also potential Pareto improvement. These improvements cause some people to gain while others to lose. With the government intervention, there are overall net gains as the gainers could compensate the losers and still be better off (Stiglitz, 1991; Akerlof, 1970; Baumol, 1952). In the neo-classical market economics, there is no way to ensure that the gainers would compensate the losers without institutionalized mechanisms to redistribute income.

It is important to note that, unlike the tax policy, where the theory of optimal taxation was developed, there is not a comparable theory of optimal expenditure policy that provides comparably well-defined rules for expenditure allocation. The key ideas of the expenditure policy were the concept of externalities and market failure that suggested only 'efficiency enhancing' interventions that corrected the underprovision of a product or service due to market failure justified government expenditure (Stefano, Anand, & Erwin, 2005; Steven, 2001). The redistributive powers of the government through expenditure, from the normative arguments, were in favor of greater equality (Rawls, 1971; Marshall, 1950). Traditionally government expenditure represents a form of government intervention designed to promote allocation efficiency through the correction of market failures redistribution of resources equitably, and promotion of economic growth and stability (Musgrave, 1959).

The effort to improve income inequality is not just morally repulsive. Many studies such as Roberto (1996), Persson and Tabellini (1994) and Alesine and Rodrik (1992) have shown that economies in which wealth is very unequally distributed may cause slower economic growth. More importantly, the survival of the economy may to a great extent depend upon social equity. If serious inequality is to persist, and no adjustments through redistribution take place, then the gap between the rich and the poor would continuously widen. As a result, social conflict may become intense and violence may begin to emerge. Moreover, in the market mechanism advocated by the neo-classic economics, there is no way to ensure that there are overall net gains in the society from any changes in the sense that the gainers from the changes could compensate the losers and still be better off. Without institutionalized mechanisms to redistribute income, market forces thus tend to expose individuals to aggregate effects.

In the meantime, one should not view the market merely as perfect where the absence of government intervention or accepting the Adam Smith theorem of the Invisible Hand would lead market forces emerging full-blown to put human society in perfect order. Such a blind belief in the naturalness, spontaneity and efficacy of the market is probably one of the most dangerous illusions. An efficient market economy cannot exist without effective legal, administrative and regulatory institutions maintained by the government. Market institutions cannot spring up automatically. Some economists believe that market institutions would spontaneously emerge from voluntary transactions between economic agents if the governments stand aside. This has never happened before and there is no reason to believe that it is going to happen now.

1.4.4   *Demand-Led Growth Theory*

The theorem of welfare economics is further supported by the demand-led growth or the so-called government-led growth theory, originated by Kaldor (1957). The demand-led growth theory argues that government spending is both a stimulant for capital investments and a source of needed social investments. High rates of growth of demand can enhance productivity and the capacity of an economy to grow at non-inflationary rates. Savings are ultimately necessary but it is faster growth that will increase savings as both consumers and firms make more money. The government led-growth theory supports government investments in public goods where government spending further supports demand, which in turn enhances productivity growth along with supply side improvements. The theory also argues that demand for goods and services must be sustained at high levels, and these require government stimulus and substantial wages. Much of the economic growth of the past generation has depended on and benefited from high levels of new government investments including high technology, the transportation system and the education system.

Empirical evidence from Robert (2007), William and Buschnagel (2007) and Cornwall and Cornwall (2001) strongly supports the government-led growth theory. They have shown that increases in output are closely associated with growing capital investment. Acceleration in the rate of economic growth would occur when additional investments lead to more output, and the output in turn stimulate more investments. Here the government effort is of critical importance in sustaining the aggregate demand for rapid economic growth. Moreover, Eisner (1986) notes that demand growth would encourage more investments, rather than drive out private investments. In this scenario, policies that stimulate demand and high wages are critical, not only to social justice but also to economic growth in the long term.

Jeff (2007) claims that we must consider the following: government budget balancing is less important than widely assumed; deficits can be justified if they result from the government investment in neglected areas with high potential financial and social returns such as early education and transportation infrastructure. The composition of the deficit matters. If more government spending develops human capital, for example, initial budget deficits are a much less serious matter. Such outlays are more akin to spending from the development budget rather than the operating budget. He added that policies that increase wages not only are a matter of social justice but can also enhance growth.

1.5   The Malaysian Issues

1.5.1   *Income Inequality and Public Expenditure*

The unity of the multiracial society in Malaysia puts income inequality between the racial groups. The Malay, Chinese and Indian as well as the rural–urban[1] disparities are of critical importance in policy formation. Unequal distribution of wealth between the different racial groups has long been a frustrating feature of the Malaysian economic development. Inherited from the racial division by economic activities and regions during colonial times, the Malays and the Indians who were known as farmers and rubber tappers mostly stayed in rural areas, while the Chinese, known as miners and merchants, mostly stayed in urban areas. Thus, the Chinese were often considered to be richer than the other races.

Since independence, economic developmental policies usually manifest the government's commitment of ensuring equitable wealth-sharing among all Malaysians – the Malays, the Chinese, the Indians and other races, and ending the identification of race based on economic functions and regions. This commitment is made upon the realization that greater equity in the distribution of income and equal opportunities for wealth creation is essential for sustaining economic growth as well as for the insurance of social stability, especially for a multi-ethnic country like Malaysia. The New Economic Policy (NEP), which was particularly introduced in 1970, was formed with two-pronged objectives – poverty eradication irrespective of race, and the restructuring of society to correct the identification of race with economic function. It marked an important milestone for further economic developmental policies. All efforts toward meeting these objectives have been made but success has been mixed.

Table 1.1 shows that the gross domestic product (GDP) in Malaysia, in real terms, has grown by an average of 6.4 percent during the 1980 to 1990 period, reaching a great height of 10.5 percent for the 1990 to 2000 period, then 6.9 percent for the 2000 to 2008 period and 5.4 percent for the 2008 to 2013 period. Rapid economic growth over the decades has made remarkable progress in reducing poverty. The incidence of poverty reduced tremendously from 49.3 percent of the population in 1970 to 12.4, 5.7 and only 0.4 percent of the population in 1992, 2004 and 2016, respectively. Nevertheless, the country's income inequality, represented by the Gini Coefficient,

Table 1.1 The Growth Rates of GDP in Malaysia (%)

Year	Growth (%)
1980–1990	6.4
1990–2000	10.5
2000–2008	6.9
2008–2013	5.4
2013–2018	5.8

Source: Ministry of Economic Affairs
Notes: All the growth rates are preliminary values.

decreased only slightly to 0.399 in 2016 after a significant fall in income inequality during the 1970s and the 1980s declined significantly to 0.446 in 1989 from 0.557 in 1976. Rising income inequality in the late 1990s and the 2000s brought about a slight decrease in income inequality over the decades (Jomo, 2006; Rasiah & Ishak, 2001; Ishak, 2000). With the new national poverty line income (PLI), which was revised from RM980 to RM2, 208 in July 2020, the poverty line and poverty rate increased from 0.4 percent in 2016 to 5.6 percent in 2019.[2] By comparison, most developed European nations that have greater income equality tend to have a Gini coefficient between 0.24 and 0.36. Although Malaysia had the high poverty rates in 2019, this does not show, however, that the actual picture of the country's socioeconomic. Instead, the poverty measurement should be broadening, especially estimating different PLIs for different household groups, which vary significantly across the country. There is a need to look the inequitable distribution of income to overcome the poverty problem.

The expectations that high economic growth would accompany low-income inequality as hypothesized by the inverted 'U-shaped' Kuznets' curve have not come true. Why did they not come true? Unlike many other studies which look at the relationship between growth and income inequality to explain this phenomenon; this book looks at the impact of public expenditure on income distribution. Public expenditure becomes a source of concern for income distribution in Malaysia as it has been used extensively to achieve income equality goals since independence. It has grown rapidly by an average of 11.3 percent per annum for the 1966 to 2008[3] period and of 3.9 percent only per annum for the 2009 to 2019[4,5] period. Public expenditure is considered a very impressive instrument for dealing with the distribution of income compared to taxation (Paternostro, Rajaram, & Tiongson, 2007; Rhee, Zhuang, Kanbur, & Felipe, 2014; Martinez-Vazquez, Moreno-Dodson, & Vulovic, 2015; Doumbia & Kinda, 2019). Indeed, efficient public expenditure means a great

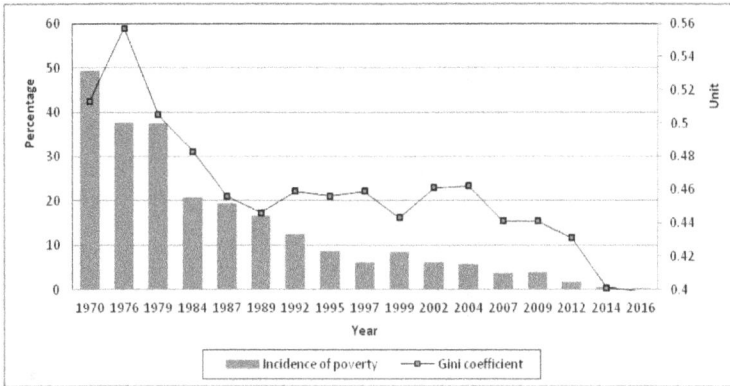

Figure 1.2 Incidence of Poverty and Income Inequality in Malaysia
Source: Ministry of Economic Affairs

deal of effort in reducing income inequality and maintaining a high level of incorporation with the globalization in developing countries (United Nations Development Programme, 2013; Rhee et al., 2014).

Malaysia reached a record high in public expenditure during the Ninth Malaysia Plan (2006–2010). This reaffirmed the commitment to improve the distribution of the fruits of further economic growth. Stronger efforts went toward addressing persistent inequalities and improving distribution. As shown in Table 1.2, the budget allocation rose to RM790.8 billion, an increase from RM559.2 billion during the Eight Malaysia Plan (2001–2005) and RM490.6 billion during the Seventh Malaysia Plan (1996–2000). Then the budget planning underwent a drastic change in the recent phase of five-year developmental plans with new ideas developed to bring Malaysia toward a high-income country by 2020. The formulation of the Tenth Malaysia Plan (2011–2015) and the Eleventh Malaysia Plan (2016–2020) closely followed the 12 National Key Economic Areas (NKEAs)[6] that were on the list of the Economic Transformation Programme (ETP) roadmap. They left out the sectoral approach adopted in traditional five-year plans to more broad strategic plans (Lee & Lee, 2017). Focusing on the sustainability of public finances, the government became prudent in mapping out the budget allocations to respond to the continued uncertainty in the global economic environment. To reach this, the budget allocation turned out to be diminished – reduced to RM747.5 billion during the Tenth Malaysia Plan and only RM519.9 billion in the recent mid-term review of the Eleventh Malaysia Plan with regard to low revenue receipts due to the highly volatile situation of the oil market condition.

Table 1.2 Federal Government Account

Item	RM Billion							Cumulative				
	1990	1995	2000	2005	2010	2015	2019	7MP	8MP	9MP	10MP	11MP
General Government												
Revenue	38.5	62.3	76.0	95.0	127.2	216.0	230.8	364.5	461.4	683.1	554.1	432.7
Operating expenditure	29.4	41.4	64.4	106.6	167.1	243.3	289.4	267.7	396.7	595.5	517.5	427.9
Current surplus/deficit	9.0	20.9	11.6	−11.7	−40.0	−27.3	−58.6	96.7	64.7	87.6	36.6	4.8
Investment expenditure	14.6	29.8	50.4	66.1	103.0	140.4	139.8	222.9	162.5	195.3	230.0	92.0
Total expenditure	44.0	71.2	114.9	172.7	270.2	383.7	429.2	490.6	559.2	790.8	747.5	519.9

Source: Eight Malaysian Plan, Ninth Malaysia Plan, Mid-term Review of the Eleventh Malaysia Plan

Notes : General government comprises federal government, state government, local authorities and statutory bodies.

Table 1.3 Proportion of the Total Federal Government Development Expenditure: A Functional Classification

	1971–1975	1976–1980	1981–1985	1986–1990	1991–1995	1996–2000	2001–2005	2006–2010	2011–2015	2015–2019[2]
Defense and security	13.5	15.8	15.1	8.3	21.7	11.7	13.3	10.9	10.5	11.5
Economic services	68.7	65.0	58.1	62.8	47.9	45.5	38.7	50.3	59.5	56.8
Agricultural and rural development	24.0	18.3	13.4	15.3	11.3	5.6	5.7	9.2	5.4	4.9
Trade and industry	18.3	15.6	14.2	15.7	8.1	12.3	9.5	11.2	13.9	10.7
Public utilities	4.2	8.5	9.5	10.5	6.5	7.6	3.7	7.0	10.2	6.8
Transportation	18.3	16.8	15.0	18.8	21.5	19.1	18.9	19.7	19.6	24.0
Others	3.9	5.8	6.0	2.4	0.3	0.9	0.9	3.2	10.4	10.4
Social services	14.9	16.3	25.1	26.1	25.8	33.0	40.5	33.5	26.7	26.7
Education	9.9	7.8	9.8	15.6	14.0	18.7	24.1	19.1	14.6	13.0
Health	2.4	1.3	1.4	2.6	4.3	3.8	5.5	4.9	4.0	3.6
Housing	1.9	5.5	11.1	3.9	2.0	4.6	4.5	4.0	2.2	3.0
Social & community services	0.7	1.7	2.8	4.0	5.5	6.0	6.4	5.6	5.9	7.1
General administration[1]	2.9	2.9	1.7	2.8	4.6	9.8	7.5	5.2	3.3	5.0

Source: Calculation based on data from Ministry of Economic Affairs, Malaysia.

Notes: 1) All figures are an average annual proportion during the period.

1 Include Public Services, Statistics, Royal Customs and Excise, Inland Revenue Departments and Ministry of Foreign Affairs.
2 Forecast.

The trend for public sector expenditure in Table 1.3 shows that the composition of expenditure throughout the years has undergone a significant change alongside the country's development process. In the early years after independence until the 1970s, expenditure on agriculture and rural development formed the largest proportion of the development expenditure. Expenditure on transportation ranked second followed by expenditure on education, trade and industry. Starting from 1980 expenditure on agriculture and rural development declined significantly and only formed a small proportion of the development expenditure. On the contrary, the expenditure on education increased significantly to form the largest proportion of the development expenditure. Expenditure on transportation, trade and industry was then higher than the expenditure on agriculture and rural development. Despite this, a resurgence of interest on the subject of regional development imbalances and bridging the urban–rural development gap in the latest mid-term review of the Eleventh Malaysia Plan expects to increase the expenditure on agriculture and rural development in later years.

1.5.2   *Public Sector and Economic Development*

The role of the public sector in economic development can be viewed in Table 1.4. Since independence, the public sector has shown an increasing role but starting from the 1980s, it declined but bounced back in the first half of the 2000s (2001–2005). Yet, it declined slightly again in the second half of the 2000s (2006–2008) and the 2010s. This was represented by an increasing proportion of the federal government expenditure of the Gross National Product (GNP) and the federal government tax revenue of the GNP during 1966–1985, a decreasing proportion during 1986–2000, an increasing proportion during 2001–2005 and a decreasing proportion during 2006–2019. The role of the public sector in the 2000s and the 2010s was relatively minor – different than in the 1970s and the 1980s.

The increasing proportion from 1966 to 1985 was due to the growth of expenditure and tax revenue at 14.4 percent and 14.7 percent, respectively, that had surpassed the growth of the GNP of 11.4 percent on average. The proportion of the federal government expenditure to the GNP had risen continuously from 23.5 percent during 1966–1970 to 40.1 percent during 1981–1985. Similarly, government tax revenue as a proportion of the GNP had also increased from 15.2 percent to 22.4 percent. This rapid growth of the expenditure and tax revenue reflected the expansion of the government to the use of the fiscal system as an instrument of growth, redistribution and stabilization. However, starting from 1985, it appeared that the public sector's role in economic development had been reduced and shifted to the private sector. The government had taken steps to reduce gradually its role and size to prevent any further strain on its financial resources (fiscal deficit at 11.3 percent during 1981–1985). These steps involved the privatization of certain government services, liberalization and deregulation to provide a more conducive environment for greater private sector activities. As a result, there was a significant cut in government expenditure in which the rate of expenditure growth declined remarkably from 21.2 percent during 1976–1980 to 9.0 percent during 1981–1985. The proportion of expenditure to the GNP, which was still high during 1981–1985 at 40.1 percent, declined to 33.3 percent during 1986–1990 and 26.7 percent during 1991–1995. Similarly, the public sector proportion of the total gross capital formation of 45.0 percent during 1981–1985 declined to 38.5 percent during 1986–1990 and 33.7 percent during 1991–1995.

The shift to an increasing role of the private sector in economy that began in the 1980s served the country well for a while. The period was marked by fast growth and a sharp fall in poverty. Although the government's role still continued focusing on the redistribution of wealth, the focus on the private sector-led growth undermined the government's redistributive capacity. This development also had other significant costs including a very high domestic bank debt as the development was financed mainly by domestic commercial banks, loosely protected industries and certain over-supportive conglomerate companies. All of these factors constrained the country's ability to adjust to a changing global environment when Thailand devaluated its currency in late 1997. Many companies went bankrupt and defaulted in paying loans. High non-performing loans and significant losses appeared in almost all bank balance sheets. More importantly, the standard of living deteriorated day by day, which caused the income inequality to widen. This scenario forced the government to take serious actions and it led to the establishment of Danamodal and Danaharta to restructure the debt, to inject new capital or to take over the dying companies.

The period therefore exhibited a shift back from the private sector-led growth to the public sector-led growth. The role of the government in economic development was increased again. The government seemed to take more control of the economy. Income equality was back as the most important agenda of the government policies, as evidence by the proportion of the total government expenditure of the GNP bounded back to 38.6 percent for the 2001–2005 period. It is almost on the same level as the 1970s period. Similarly the proportion of the government tax revenue of the GNP rose back to the 1970s' level. More significant was the increase in the proportion of public sector investment of the total gross capital formation leveling at around from 35 percent during 1986–2000 to 59.5 percent during 2001–2005. This left the private sector investment accounting only for 40.5 percent of the total gross capital formation.

In addition, the openness of the Malaysian economy increased its susceptibility to the Global Financial Crisis in 2008 due to the subprime mortgage crisis in the United States (US). The country was struck by a serious deterioration in external demand and private investment. The government took steps to boost domestic demand through expeditious fiscal injections. More importantly, the government became more prudent in budget allocation to increase the fiscal flexibility in response to any contingency, given the continued uncertainty of the global economy. The role of the private sector in the economy had reemphasized since then, focusing upon a skillful and talented workforce, extensive research and development (R&D) activities and the cultivation of innovative surroundings. As a consequence, the proportion of the total expenditure of the GNP reduced constantly to 37.9, 37.1 and 30.4 percent for the 2006–2019 period, while the proportion of tax revenue of the GNP reduced quite significantly to 17.8 percent during 2006–2010 and 17.6 percent during 2016–2019, even though it appeared to be high during 2011–2015 at about 20 percent with the goods and services taxes (GSTs), which came into effect on April 2015. The proportion of the public sector investment of the total gross capital formation also reduced significantly to 39.1 percent and the private sector investment appeared to be high at 61 percent on average.

To give a light and general view of the public sector financial performance (detailed analysis is in Chapter 2), Table 1.4 shows that the federal government registered a surplus of 0.1 percent of the GNP during 1991–1995 and a lower deficit at 1.6 percent during 1996–2000 before reaching a surplus of 2.0 percent during 2001–2005. Low deficits were further on the path with 3.7 percent during 2006–2010, 5.8 percent during 2011–2015 and 4.7 percent during 2016–2019 compared to the previous periods – a deficit of 5.1 percent during 1966–1970, 7.8 percent during 1971–1975, 6.2 percent during 1976–1980 and 11.3 percent during 1981–1985.

Looking back at the pre-crisis period in the early 1990s, the government accounts registered a surplus as a result of the government merely assuming a supportive role in the development process. However, in response to the 1997 financial crisis, the government introduced measures to prevent further economic contractions and a decline in the standard of living, which brought the government to a deficit of 6.0 percent of the GNP in 2000 from a surplus of 2.4 percent in 1994. The deficit was mainly contributed by a significant increase in the government expenditure from RM41.8 billion in 1994 to RM68.2 billion in 2000. The deficit of the federal government however enhanced and reached a surplus of 1.45 percent of the GNP in 2005. This was particularly due to the high growth of the government tax revenue, which recorded an annual growth rate of 5.6 percent during 2001–2005 compared with only 3.1 percent during 1996–2000. The higher revenue received by the federal government particularly was from the higher

Table 1.4 Key Indicators of Public Sector

	1966–1970	1971–1975	1976–1980	1981–1985	1986–1990	1991–1995	1996–2000	2001–2005	2006–2010	2011–2015	2016–2019*
Growth rate of GNP	6.3	13.6	18.3	7.8	10.0	13.2	8.3	10.1	6.7	5.4	5.5
Growth rate of total revenue	8.7	17.1	22.3	8.8	7.7	11.7	4.5	5.2	4.5	6.1	1.3
Growth rate of tax revenue	9.1	19.2	23.4	6.9	6.3	14.5	3.1	5.6	4.8	4.2	1.0
Growth rate of total expenditure	7.2	20.1	21.2	9.0	7.1	7.3	11.0	5.7	5.8	5.2	2.0
Tax revenue/GNP	15.2	17.3	21.4	22.4	18.1	19.9	17.5	25.2	17.8	19.5	17.6
Expenditure/GNP	23.5	29.4	31.7	40.1	33.3	26.7	24.4	38.6	37.9	37.1	30.4
Government deficit/GNP	−5.1	−7.8	−6.2	−11.3	−5.9	0.1	−1.6	2.0	−3.7	−5.8	−4.7
Public gross capital formation/total gross capital formation	36.9	31.4	36.3	45.0	38.5	33.7	39.2	59.5	46.4	39.1	31.7
Private gross capital formation/total gross capital formation	63.1	68.6	63.7	55.0	61.5	66.3	60.8	40.5	53.6	60.9	68.3

Source: Calculation based on data from Malaysia Economic Report (various years), BNM Quarterly Bulletin (various issues) and Ministry of Economic Affairs, Malaysia (www.mea.gov.my/en/economic-statistics/public-sector).

Note: * Forecast.

dividends paid by PETRONAS and the higher tax revenue from the company and individual income taxes as well as import duties and excise duties.

At the present time, the dominance of petroleum-related tax makes the government's receipt increasingly difficult day by day. It is not only a matter of the depletion of the oil resource, but also the highly volatile world oil prices that would greatly impact public finance. The tax revenues have shrunk immensely with a great fall in world oil prices to under $50 per barrel in January 2015 after being held at a fairly stable high level at around $110 per barrel from 2010 to mid-2014. This led to a high fiscal deficit of 5.8 percent during 2011–2015 and 4.7 percent during 2016–2019 due to the diminishing yield in the oil resource. The fiscal deficit, which has grown steadily worse, was recorded at 3.7 percent during 2006–2010, although the government had undertaken a few fiscal reform programs such as the abolition of fuel subsidies, which took effect from 2014 and the introduction of GST in 2015.

An analysis of the consolidated public sector comprising the federal government, the state government, the statutory body and the local government is to provide a more complete picture of the issues. Among the institutions, the federal government is the most predominant in almost every aspect of the development of economics: planning, functioning and financing. As the federal government carries the main burden of expenditure for the economy, it pays for the salaries and pensions of civil servants, defense and internal security, education and health services, and land and rural development. The state governments control various aspects of agriculture and forestry, mining and religious matters. The autonomy of the state governments in these various activities, however, is restricted by the activities of the federal authority, particularly the federal land and development authority. Therefore, the extent of government involvement in the economy has gained more attention recently, as economy today has grown in both size and complexity to an unprecedented level. The central question is not whether government involvement is good or bad, but more to whether a heavier role of the government is necessary along with market competition in allocating resources and determining incomes.

1.6   Conclusions

The economic growth of a country can only be sustained when including the distribution of both the income and the wealth of the population. Here comes the potential role for the government to work at a steady pace with economic growth while improving the distribution of income within a society. Theoretical works like Kuznets' 'Inverted U Theory,' the competitive market theory and the demand-led growth theory have put great emphasis on government interventions to correct the market failures to maximize the pleasures of the society. From Hari Merdeka (Malaysia's Independence Day) to the present day, the income disparity of the country, irrespective of race and region, is always at the top of the agenda for the government. Various measures and policies were introduced and imposed in the hope of narrowing the gap of income disparities, but still the expectation of high economic growth, partnered with low-income inequality as hypothesized by the inverted 'U-shaped' Kuznets' curve, could not succeed. Thus, an analysis of public expenditure expansion by total and by different groups becomes critical, especially when the current economy becomes more challenging.

Notes

1 Household Income Survey (HIS) defined 'urban areas' as those towns with a population of at least 10,000 inhabitants while those areas with a population of fewer than 10,000 inhabitants were defined as rural areas.
2 The method of poverty line for Malaysia hadn't been updated since 2005.
3 Calculation based on data from Bank Negara Malaysia (BNM) Quarterly Bulletin (various issues).
4 Forecast.
5 Calculation based on the table of consolidated public sector from the Ministry of Economic Affairs, Malaysia.
6 12 NKEAs highlighted on agriculture; palm oil and related products; oil, gas and energy; electrical and electronics; wholesale and retail; education; healthcare; communication content and infrastructure; tourism; financial services as well as business services.

References

Akerlof, G. A. (1970). The market for "lemons": Quality uncertainty and the market mechanism. *The Quarterly Journal of Economics, 84*(3), 488–500.
Alesine, A., & Rodrik, D. (1992). Distribution, political conflict and economic growth. In A. Cukierman, Z. Hercowitz, & L. Leiderman (Eds.), *Political economy, growth and business cycles* (pp. 23–50). Cambridge, MA: MIT Press.
Baumol, W. J. (1952). The transactions demand for cash: An inventory theoretic approach. *The Quarterly Journal of Economics, 66*(4), 545–556.
Cornwall, J., & Cornwall, W. (2001). *Capitalist development in the twentieth century: An evolutionary Keynesian analysis*. Cambridge: Cambridge University Press.
Dollar, D., & Kraay, A. (2002). Growth is good for the poor. *Journal of Economic Growth, 7*, 195–225.
Doumbia, D., & Kinda, T. (2019). *Reallocating public spending to reduce income inequality: Can it work.* IMF Working Paper WP/19/188? Retrieved from www.imf.org/en/Publications/WP/Issues/2019/09/06/Reallocating-Public-Spending-to-Reduce-Income-Inequality-Can-It-Work-48607
Eisner, R. (1986). *How real is the Federal deficit?* New York: New York Press.

Gustafsson, B., & Johansson, M. (1999). In search of smoking guns: What makes income inequality vary over time in different countries? *American Sociological Review, 64*(4), 585–605.

Ishak, S. (2000). Economic growth and income inequality in Malaysia, 1971–1995. *Journal of the Asia Pacific Economy, 5*(1&2).

Jeff, M. (2007). *Breaking the stranglehold on growth. Why policies promoting demand offer a better way for the U.S economy* (EPI Briefing Paper, 192). Retrieved from https://www.epi.org/publication/bp192/.

Jomo, K.S. (2006). *Growth with equity in East Asia* (DESA Working Paper No.33). New York: Economics & Social Affairs.

Kaldor, N. (1957). A model of economic growth. *The Economic Journal, 67*(268), 591–624.

Kuznets, S. (1956). Economic growth and income inequality. *American Economic Review, 45*, 1–28.

Lee, C., & Lee, C. G. (2017). The evolution of development planning in Malaysia. *Journal of Southeast Asian Economies, 34*(3), 436–461.

Malaysia. (1996). *Seventh Malaysia plan 1996–2000*. Kuala Lumpur: National Printing Department.

Malaysia. (1999). *Household income survey 1998/1999*. Unpublished. Kuala Lumpur: Department of Statistics.

Malaysia. (2001). *Eight Malaysia plan 2001–2005*. Kuala Lumpur: National Printing Department.

Malaysia. (2010). *Tenth Malaysia plan 2011–2015*. Kuala Lumpur: National Printing Department.

Malaysia. (2015). *Eleventh Malaysia plan 2016–2020*. Kuala Lumpur: National Printing Department.

Malaysia. (2010). *Economic transformation programme*. Kuala Lumpur: Prime Minister's Department.

Marshall, T. H. (1950). *Citizenship and social class and other essays*. Cambridge: Cambridge University Press.

Martinez-Vazquez, J., Moreno-Dodson, B., & Vulovic, V. (2015). *The impact of tax and expenditure policies on income distribution: Evidence from a large panel of countries* (International Center for Public Policy's Working Paper 12–25). Atlanta, Georgia: Georgia State University.

Musgrave, R. (1959). *The theory of public finance*. New York: McGraw-Hill.

Oppenheim, C. (1993). *Poverty: The facts*. London: Bath Press.

Paternostro, S., Rajaram, A., & Tiongson, E. R. (2007). How does the composition of public spending matter? *Oxford Development Studies, 35*(1), 47–82.

Pattnaik, R. K., Bose, D., Bhattacharyya, I., & Chander, J. (2006). *Public expenditure and emerging fiscal policy scenario in India*. Mumbai, Maharashtra: Reserve Bank of India.

Persson, T., & Tabellini, G. (1994). Is inequality harmful for growth? *American Economic Review, 84*, 600–621.

Rasiah, R., & Ishak, S. (2001). Market, government and Malaysia's new economic policy. *Cambridge Journal of Economics, 25*, 57–58.

Rawls, J. (1971). *A theory of justice*. Cambridge, MA: Harvard University Press.

Rhee, C. Y., Zhuang, J. Z., Kanbur, R., & Felipe, J. (2014). Confronting Asia's rising inequality: Policy option. In R. Kanbur, C. Y. Rhee, & J. Z. Zhuang (Eds.), *Inequality in Asia and the Pacific: Trends, drivers, and policy implications* (pp. 79–100). Manila, Philippines: Asian Development Bank.

Robert, L. (2007). *Enriching children, enriching the nation: Public investment in high quality prekindergarten*. Washington, DC: Economic Policy Institute.

Roberto, P. (1996). Growth, income distribution and democracy: What the data say. *Journal of Economic Growth, 1*, 149–187.

Rowntree, B. S. (1901). *Poverty: A study of town life*. London: Macmillan.

Stefano, P., Anand, R., & Erwin, R. T. (2005). How does the composition of public spending matter? *Policy Research Working Paper*, 3555. Washington, DC: The World Bank.

Steven, E. L. (2001). *Price theory and applications*. Nashville, US: South-Western College Publishing.

Stiglitz, J. E. (1991). The invisible hand and modern welfare economics. *NBER Working Papers Series*, 3641. Cambridge, MA: National Bureau of Economic Research.

United Nations Development Programme. (2013). *Humanity divided: Confronting inequality in developing countries*. New York: UNDP.

William, D., & Buschnagel, C. (2007). *Dynamic estimates of fiscal effects of investing in preschool education*. Washington, DC: Brooking Institutions.

2 Malaysian Economy, Income Distribution and Public Expenditure

2.1 Introduction

This chapter presents some important features and characteristics of the Malaysian economy on account of the income distribution analysis. Moreover, the structure and the trend in public sector expenditure are reviewed to identify the scope for a restrained income distribution in such expenditure. Sections 2.2 and 2.3 review the Malaysian economic performance and its society. Section 2.4 looks at the policies on poverty and income distribution. Section 2.5 considers the trends in poverty and income inequality in the country over the past 30 years, specifically focusing on income shares, mean monthly household incomes, the Gini coefficient, ownership of the share capital of limited companies and the distribution of employment. Section 2.6 discusses the general structure and the trends in public sector expenditure with two specific sub-sections on current expenditure and development expenditure. Section 2.7 approaches the direction of changes in the public sector budget management throughout the 1964 to 2018 period. Lastly, Section 2.8 includes the concluding remarks of the chapter.

2.2 Review of the Malaysian Economic Performance

Malaysia has made significant achievements in developing its economy and improving the quality of life of its people. As shown in Table 1.1, the real GDP has grown by an average of 7.0 percent per annum throughout the 1980 to 2018 period. During 1980–1990, 1990–2000, 2000–2008, 2008–2013 and 2013–2018, the average annual growth rates were 6.4 percent, 10.5 percent, 6.9 percent, 5.4 percent and 5.8 percent, respectively. There were three major departures from the record of rapid growth over the period. The early one was the mid-1980s, when Malaysia experienced a brief mild recession, while the others were the more serious crises of 1997–1998 and

DOI: 10.4324/9781003302506-2

2008–2009. Yet, the country showed great courage and resilience from getting into a harsh and prolonged period of negative growth. Within the same period, there was a substantial improvement in the people's quality of life. Widespread advances were made primarily in education, infrastructure, health and industry. The population became increasingly urbanized and educated while the middle-income group expanded.

Malaysia's macroeconomic management has been among the best in the developing world. Inflation has never been a problem in most years, falling below 5 percent from 1980 onwards; and the unemployment rate was very low at below 4 percent from 1990 onwards (Table 2.1). The country is moderately indebted, as indicated by its external debt/GNP ratio of 32.9 percent in 2008 in which medium- and long-term debts accounted for almost 70 percent of the total external debt, and 67.0 percent in 2018 with about 60 percent for the medium- and long-term debts of the total external debt. Debt service which recorded an average of 5.2 percent of exports of goods and services for the 2000–2008 period has never been a problem. Remarkably among developing countries, it has never experienced a serious debt or balance of payment crisis, apart from the special case of the 1997–1998 Asian and 2008–2009 Global Financial Crises. Although the proportion of public consumption of the GNP declined from 17 percent in 1965 to 12.9 percent in 2008, it rebounded from the decline in 2013. Similarly, the proportion of private consumption of the GNP declined from 64.9 percent in 1965 to 46.7 percent in 2008 but bounced back from the decline in 2018. The proportion of private consumption of the GNP, however, was much higher than the proportion of public consumption of the GNP throughout the 1965 to 2018 period.

The Malaysian economy is exceptionally open. It is the 19th largest trading nation in the world with trade in excess of RM1 trillion. Table 2.2 shows that total trade expanded at an average rate of 12.23 percent per annum from RM8,473 million in 1965 to RM1,360,025 million in 2008 and 3.04 percent from 2008 to RM1,891,043 million in 2018. The high growth of the total trade was contributed by the growth of both exports and imports. Exports of goods and services grew by 12.49 percent per annum for the period 1965 (RM4,307 million) to 2008 (RM765,370 million) and by 2.43 percent for the period 2008 to 2018 (RM996,352 million). The strong export growth has been a major lead for the rapid expansion of the economy. Table 2.1 shows that the export of goods and services constituted 106.7 percent of the GNP in 2008 and 72.2 percent of the GNP in 2018, while it accounted for only 49 percent of the GNP in 1965. As a proportion of the total growth, electric and electronic goods grew significantly, becoming the most valuable exported products, while, primary exports, particularly rubber and tin fell sharply. On the other hand, the import of goods and services constituted

Table 2.1 Various Important Economic Indicators for Malaysia

	1965	1970	1975	1980	1985	1990	1995	2000	2005	2008	2013	2018ᵖ
GNP at market prices (RM billion)	8.6	11.6	21.6	49.9	71.9	114.0	212.1	314.3	495.5	717.2	984.8	1380.5
Percent of GNP												
Private consumption	64.9	64.3	55.8	60.0	55.9	54.1	50.3	46.2	47.1	46.7	53.6	59.4
Public consumption	17.0	18.6	18.2	17.6	16.5	14.4	12.9	11.4	12.9	12.9	14.2	12.3
Private fixed capital formation	9.1	12.5	16.2	21.6	17.1	21.2	32.7	14.0	9	11.1	16.5	17.8
Public fixed capital formation	7.3	5.9	9.8	11.6	15.1	11.7	13.0	13.9	11.0	9.0	10.9	7.4
Increase in stocks	0	2.7	−0.09	−0.12	−2.4	−0.7	0.06	1.9	−0.4	−0.2	−0.6	−0.8
Export of goods and services	49.0	48.1	48.7	64.7	59.1	77.8	98.7	135.9	123.3	106.7	78.2	72.2
Import of goods and services	−47.4	−46.4	−53.2	−65.9	−53.6	−75.6	−102.8	−114.1	−99.8	−82.9	−69.4	−64.8
Net factor payment paid abroad	0.1	−5.7	4.59	−9.5	−7.7	−2.9	−4.9	−9.2	−3.1	−3.3	−3.4	3.6
Total	100	100	100	100	100	100	100	100	100	100	100	100
Per capita GNP (RM)	920	1169	1840	3763	4580	6299	10252	13378	18966	25784	32596	42627
Saving/GNP	17.4	22.0	22.8	30.8	29.3	31.6	35.6	40.1	36.5	38.0	30.4	26.9
Rate of inflation (%)	-	1.9	-	3.4*	0.3	2.6	3.4	1.6	3.0	5.4	2.1	1.0
Unemployment rate (%)	-	-	-	5.7	6.9	5.1	2.8	3.1	3.5	3.3	3.1	3.4

Source: Calculation based on data from BNM Quarterly Bulletin (various issues).

Notes: * For year 1982.
p preliminary

Table 2.2 Fixed Capital Formation and Trade

	1965 (RM million)	2008 (RM million)	2018 (RM million)	Average annual growth rate (%)	
				1965–2008	2008–2018
Total fixed capital formation	1,664	1,44,635	3,48,866	10.68	8.33
Public fixed capital formation	626	64,834	2,46,410	11.12	12.91
Private fixed capital formation	1,038	79,801	102,456	10.37	2.3
Total trade	8,473	1,360,025	1,891,043	12.23	3.04
Export of goods and services	4,307	765,370	996,352	12.49	2.43
Import of goods and services	4,166	594,655	894,691	11.94	3.78

Source: BNM Quarterly Bulletin (various issues), Malaysia Economic Report 2008/2009.

Notes: Calculation based on data BNM Quarterly Bulletin (various issues), Malaysia Economic Report 2008/2009.

82.9 percent of the GNP in 2008 and 64.8 percent of the GNP in 2018, while it accounted for only 47.4 percent of the GNP in 1965 (Table 2.1). The high demand for import was for intermediate and capital goods, particularly for industrial development.

Apart from that, the total gross fixed capital formation of the country increased at 10.68 percent per annum for the period 1965 (RM1,664 million) to 2008 (RM144,635 million) and at 8.0 percent per annum for the period 2008 to 2018 (RM348,866 million) (Table 2.2). This was attributed to a significant increase in both the public and the private fixed capital formation. The annual growth rates of the public and the private fixed capital formation were 11.12 percent and 10.37 percent for the 1965–2008 period, as well as 12.91 percent and 2.3 percent for the 2008–2018 period, respectively. In fact, the proportion of the public fixed capital formation of the GNP was lower than the private fixed capital formation for almost all years except for 2005 (Table 2.1). The proportion of the public fixed capital formation of the GNP was 11 percent in 2005, slightly higher than 9.0 percent of the proportion of the private fixed capital formation. The higher proportion was probably due to the counter-cyclical measures adopted by the government to control the impact of the 1997 recession.

The high economic growth of this period was accompanied by a structural transformation of the economy as pictured in Table 2.3. A significant

Table 2.3 Sector Share of GDP

Year	Manufacturing/ GDP (Pct)	Agriculture/ GDP (Pct)	Services/ GDP (Pct)
1970	12.0	29.0	–
1980	21.0	22.0	40.0
1990	24.6	16.3	44.1
1995	27.1	10.3	47.7
2000	31.9	8.9	49.9
2005	30.7	8.0	48.1
2010	27.6	7.3	54.6
2015	22.3	8.3	52.0
2016	22.3	7.6	52.6
2017*	22.3	7.6	52.9
2018P	22.4	7.3	54.0

Source: Ministry of Economic Affairs, Malaysia.

Notes: * Estimated.
P Preliminary.

transformation occurred in the composition of the sectoral output. The contribution of the manufacturing and the services sectors increased at the expense of the agricultural sector. Over the 1970–2018 period, the share of agriculture to the GDP fell quickly from 29 percent to 7.3 percent. Most of the increase occurred in manufacturing, which almost tripled its share from 12 percent to 30.7 percent in 2005 and almost doubled to 22.4 percent in 2018. Manufacturing output surpassed that of agriculture in the late 1980s, and is now almost four times larger. Growth in the manufacturing sector was led by resource-based industries, which recorded an average growth of 5.0 percent per annum. The share of the services sector rose significantly since the late 1990s. For the 2000–2018 period, the services sector was the major contributor to GDP growth, growing at an average annual rate of 9.3 percent. Its share of the GDP increased to 54.6 percent in 2010 and was maintained at around 52 percent before increasing to 54 percent in 2018.

Along with the structural changes, significant changes have also occurred within the major sectors in the economy. The primary sector of the early post-independence years consisted mainly of rubber, tin and mining. Since the 1980s, palm oil has caught up rubber in terms of the value of production and exports. Meanwhile, the manufacturing sector saw a significant expansion of industries producing electrical and electronic equipment, agro-based manufacturing, petroleum products and textiles. The finance, insurance, real estate and business services were the leading sub-sectors for the services sector, which contributed the highest growth at an average rate of 8.1 percent per annum within the period. Employment shares also changed significantly, albeit not as fast. From 1975 to 2006, the agricultural share of employment fell by more than half, while that of manufacturing rose by about 50 percent. Manufacturing employment overtook agriculture in the mid-1990s. In 2006, a total of 1.4 billion individuals or 12.9 percent of the total labor force was involved in the agriculture sector. Of this total labor, about 50 percent were agricultural operators, 40 percent were workers and 10 percent were unpaid family workers. Nevertheless, the growth in the service sector outpaced that of the goods-producing sector making it overtake manufacturing, employing the majority of workers with about 60 percent of the total labor force for the recent ten years. This trend is expected to be continued in the service-based sector, and high-value manufacturing is now at the top of the agenda to promote sustainable economic growth.

Despite the declining agricultural share of the GDP, the sector continued to provide the raw materials required by the domestic agro-based industries and part of the nation's food demand. In the Ninth Malaysia Plan, the agricultural sector was revitalized to become the third engine of growth after services and manufacturing. The emphasis involved enlarging the commercial farming scale, widening the application of new technology, producing high-quality and value-added products, improving biotechnology and communication technology, and encouraging the participation of entrepreneurial farmers and skilled workers. With the growing importance of agriculture, particularly in food security and strengthening the domestic supply chain, the sector continued to stay focused in recent policy documents such as the Tenth (10MP) and the Eleventh Malaysia Plans (11MP), the National Food Security Policy, the National Agro-food Policy and the National Commodity Policy. Agriculture became one among the 12 potentials of the NKEAs aimed to boost the country's economic foundation with a steady income growth. In the recent Eleventh Malaysia Plan, the agriculture sector was sought to be transformed and modernized into a high-income and sustainable sector, taking account of the sustainable agricultural practices and the adoption of modern technologies.

As one of the most open economies in the world, external events quickly gave impacts to the Malaysian economy. Nevertheless, when the economy experienced difficulty from external shocks, for example, in the 2008–2009 global financial crisis, the 1997–1998 Asian economic crisis and the mid-1980s recession, it has invariably bounced back quickly, which testifies to its fundamental strengths and resilience.

2.3   Background of the Malaysian Society

Malaysia is a multiethnic society with three major ethnic groups, namely, Malays, Chinese and Indians. In 2018, the total population was 32.4 million persons. The Bumiputera, most of whom are Malays, accounted for 69.1 percent of the population, while the Chinese and the Indians accounted for 23.0 percent and 6.9 percent, respectively.[1] Other races accounted for 1.0 percent of the population.

Malaysia inherited a multiracial society from the British colonial rule. During the colonial rule, a large number of Chinese were brought to Malaysia to work in the mining industry and a large number of Indians were brought to work in the rubber plantations and rail roads, while the Malays continued to work in the traditional agricultural activities. This resulted in a significant change in the ethnic composition of Malaysia. The ethnic groups started to be identified on the basis of the economic activities and were separated by geographical locations. At the time of independence, the majority of the Malays lived in the underdeveloped rural areas, and were involved in traditional agricultural activities. The majority of the Chinese lived in relatively developed urban areas. A marked income inequality existed between the Malays, the Chinese and the Indians. Until today, this income inequality still exists between the Malays, the Chinese and the Indians, where the Malays work in agricultural activities in rural areas and the non-Malays work in non-agricultural activities in urban areas.

2.4   Policies on Poverty and Income Distribution in Malaysia

The government of Malaysia formulated a range of national development policies during 1970–2008. The major policies can be broadly categorized as the NEP, the National Development Policy (NDP) and Vision 2020. All these three policies embodied the philosophy of the Malaysian government of economic growth with zero poverty and income equality.

The NEP was introduced in 1970 as the government intended to overcome the perceived imbalances in the society at that time. The NEP was to be implemented in the span of 20 years from 1970 to 1990. The policy program was committed to poverty eradication and greater inter-ethnic parity via redistribution, via its two main objectives (a) to reduce and eventually eradicate poverty by raising income levels and increasing employment opportunities among all Malaysians, irrespective of race and (b) to restructure the Malaysian society to correct economic imbalances to reduce and eventually eliminate the identification of race by economic functions. The policy stressed on the socio-economic development of the Malays.

Through the NEP, Malaysia deepened its agricultural and rural area development efforts such as the Green Revolution in rice cultivation, which involved double cropping, green revolutionary strains, fertilizers, plugging and harvesting machinery. There was a land reform where new agricultural areas, distributed through land development schemes, were managed by government agencies such as the Federal Land Development Authority (FELDA), Federal Land Consolidation and Rehabilitation Authority (FELCRA) and the Rubber Industry Smallholders Development Authority (RISDA). Besides, extensive investments to develop infrastructure in rural areas, special ministries and government agencies, such as the Malaysian Agricultural Research and Development Institute (MARDI), Bank Bumiputera, Majlis Amanah Rakyat (MARA) and Pernas, were also set up to enhance the socio-economic standing of the Malays.

To restructure society and achieve an equitable distribution of income, various affirmative actions for the Malay community were implemented to increase their participation in business and employment, particularly done through their participation in education. In the government's efforts to nurture a Bumiputera Commercial and Industrial Community (BCIC), specific programs were carried out to promote Malay entrepreneurs and their participation in the commercial and industrial sectors. An equity ownership target of at least 30 percent for the Bumiputera (most of them were Malays) by 1990 was incorporated in the NEP.

The NDP, which succeeded the NEP in 1991, was implemented during the 1991–2000 period. The NDP indicated a shift from the NEP's emphasis on redistribution to growth with a marked reduction in the role of the public sector. This was due to the fact that by 1990, the problem of poverty was not as serious as it was in 1970. Therefore, in dealing with the remaining problems of poverty, the NDP shifted its focus toward the eradication of hardcore poverty. The income equality strategy was implemented through creating more employment opportunities and more participation of the Bumiputera in the industrial sector. The main objective of the NDP to attain high economic growth was to be achieved by relying more on the private sector, particularly for industrialization through increasing productivity, using higher technology and better quality products. The public sector only played a supportive and complementary role.

Vision 2020's Third Outline Perspective Plan (OPP3) succeeded the NDP when it came to an end in 2000. Vision 2020 provided the general thrust of Malaysia's development strategy for the 2001–2010 period to achieve the long-term objectives of becoming a fully developed nation by 2020. Vision 2020 extended the NDP objective of rapid economic growth through rapid industrialization but gave more emphasis on diversifying the manufacturing base, developing small- and medium-scale industries, promoting inter-industry linkages and developing human resources. In order to balance the economic growth, emphasis was also given to the development of the agricultural and the service sectors.

Under OPP3, the Ninth Malaysia Plan (2006–2010) provided the thrust to address persistent socio-economic inequalities constructively and productively. The approach toward addressing socio-economic imbalances focused on capacity building and raising competitiveness, and was refined to take into account the lessons learnt from past implementations as well as the pressure from global competition and liberalization. Past policies and programs were reviewed to evaluate their effectiveness and improve their future impact.

The key priorities in the Ninth Malaysia Plan were on hardcore poverty eradication, overall poverty reduction and reduction in inter- and intra-ethnic inequalities. Inter- and intra-ethnic inequalities were addressed through efforts to narrow the rural–urban and regional gaps as well as the disparities in employment, income and wealth. Efforts to eradicate poverty emphasized self-help and enhancing income generation among poor households. Direct financial assistance was allocated for the elderly, the disabled and the destitute. Existing programs and projects under the *Skim Pembangunan Kesejahteraan Rakyat*, the Integrated Development Program for Urban Communities, *Amanah Ikhtiar Malaysia* and many other programs were enhanced to ensure effectiveness in lifting households out of poverty.

In view of the widening income inequalities, a more serious effort was undertaken to reduce income disparity in the Ninth Malaysia Plan. Efforts to improve income distribution focused on reducing income disparity between the Bumiputera and the non-Bumiputera ethnic groups, between rural and urban areas, between less developed and more developed regions and increasing the income of those in the bottom 40 percent income group. To reduce the disparities between the rural and urban areas, the government increased the allocation for rural development. Another approach to reducing income disparity was to improve ethnic participation in all occupational levels and sectors. Measures were also taken to encourage greater support for equal opportunity and workplace diversity among employers. In addition, measures were taken to enhance Bumiputera asset and wealth ownership. The Urban Development Authority (UDA) spearheaded efforts to improve Bumiputera property ownership in urban areas. Measures were also taken to expand competitive Bumiputera commercial enterprises, particularly small- and medium-scale enterprises. The development of the BCIC continued to be a key approach to restructuring the society.

The National Transformation Programme (NTP) came to the fore in October 2010 in the midst of a challenging world economic outlook throughout much of the year. The country began to lose the momentum of growth with increasingly intense competition in international markets, which interfered with low domestic productivity growth, and it was the time Malaysia was stuck in the middle-income trap. Despite the previous productive strategies, an innovation-led economic transformation that was driven by high labor productivity growth and investment in advanced technologies became the best way to move the country out of the slower growth path. Significantly, inequality became the pressing challenge for Malaysia at the time. Poverty eradication attempts were no longer applicable with a significant reduction of the poverty rate from about 50 percent in 1970 to almost 20 percent in 1987 and only 3.6 percent was recorded in 2007 despite the post-crisis slower growth. Nevertheless, the overall income disparity, which was measured in Gini coefficient, improved slightly from 0.459 in 1997 to 0.441 in 2007 after a significant fall in the overall Gini coefficient during the 1970s and the 1980s. In other words, the gap between the rich and the poor was still broad in the country where a large concentration of wealth was at the top.

The NTP was to become a great stepping stone to direct Malaysia to a high-income and advanced nation based upon three very critical elements, which were high income, inclusiveness and sustainability. The New Economic Model (NEM), the Economic Transformation Programme (ETP), and the Government Transformation Programme (GTP) were undertaken to ensure balanced development in the future. The NEM that was first unveiled on 30 March 2010 marked an important economic milestone after the formulation of the NEP in 1970. A package of measures put forward number of strategic reforms to transform the country into a *market-led, well-governed*, regionally integrated, *entrepreneurial* and *innovative* economy status in the future. Besides, the ETP specifically aimed to accelerate the gross national income (GNI), investment and jobs through the 12 NKEAs.[2] Public investment and policy support further prioritized these 12 NKEAs that were expected to have substantial contributions in generating high income for the nation. Meanwhile, the integration of the GTP with the formulation of the National Key Result Areas (NKRAS)[3] was based on the people's needs and wants to gain economic momentum.

The philosophy of transformation spurred the following 10th Malaysia Plan (10MP) and the 11th Malaysia Plan (11th MP) where an inclusive development approach was adopted to widen the role of community participation. The community was sought to fully benefit from the wealth of the country. The emphasis was specifically on financing instruments that would pool and mobilize funds flexibly and the earnings would go back to the people. It is interesting to note that the income levels of the bottom 40 percent households[4] and the disadvantaged segments with particular needs such as the Bumiputera in Sabah and Sarawak, the ethnic minorities and the *Orang Asli* communities in Peninsular Malaysia were appealing in the list. The households within this category had the slowest growth of average income, especially those in the rural areas, accentuating the less-than-satisfactory distribution of wealth. In the long run, this would undermine economic and social sustainability. Thus, specific supports and resources were directed to them, irrespective of ethnicity or location. The government made an approach to upgrade their education and skills through capacity enhancement programs. Besides, efforts had been made to enhance the productivity and sustainability of self-employment, micro-businesses and small-scale industries. Other than that, the Bumiputera development agenda was continued to be a major thrust by emphasizing broad-based, meaningful and sustainable economic participation for the Bumiputera. Besides strengthening Bumiputera entrepreneurship in high-impact sectors, their wealth ownership was sought to broaden beyond corporate equity, in particular expand upon properties and business assets like retail space, landed properties and intellectual properties through the pooling of funds and institutional investment.

2.5   Trends in Poverty and Income Inequality

Malaysia's development policies were implemented effectively. Starting with the good NEP policies in the 1970s, poverty continuously declined over the next decades. Besides good government policies, falling poverty levels had been accompanied by remarkable economic growth and structural changes over the previous decades. The impacts of good government policies, remarkable growth and structural change in inequality, however, were much less clear. Income inequality was reduced marginally and, in fact, was rising in recent years.

It is indicated in Table 2.4 that the incidence of poverty declined sharply for the 1970 to 1984 period, declined slowly for the 1984 to 1990 period and declined significantly for the 1990 to 2007 period. Poverty incidence declined significantly from 52.4 percent of the population in 1970 to 20.4 percent in 1984, to 16.5 percent in 1990 and to 3.6 percent in 2007. A similar trend in the incidence of poverty in urban areas was recorded. It declined significantly from 21.3 percent of the population in the urban areas in 1970 to 8.5 percent in 1984, to 7.5 percent in 1990 and to 2.0 percent in 2007. Similarly the incidence of poverty in rural areas declined significantly from 58.7 percent of the population in the rural areas in 1970 to 27.3 percent in 1984, to 21.8 percent in 1990 and to 7.1 percent in 2007. The incidence of poverty among the ethnic groups, namely, the Malays, the Chinese and the Indians also declined sharply. The incidence of poverty among the Malays, which was 65.9 percent of the Malay population in 1970, declined to 7.3 percent in 2002, while the incidence of poverty among the Chinese and the Indian population, which was 27.5 percent of the Chinese population and 40.2 percent of the Indian population, respectively, in 1970, declined to 1.5 percent and 1.9 percent in 2002. The incidence of poverty continued to fall and was virtually eradicated during the following period of 2007 to 2016 with only 0.4 percent of the population in 2016. In the meantime, only 0.2 percent of the population in the urban areas lived below the poverty line, while 1 percent lived in poverty in the rural areas. Additionally, the incidence of poverty by ethnicity had also become favorable. Poverty rates by ethnicity were somewhat very narrow with only 0.5 percent of the Malay population and 0.1 percent for both the Chinese population and the Indian population in 2016.

Table 2.4 also shows that the trends in income inequality are unclear. It seems to suggest declining inequality in the 1970s and the 1980s, and increasing inequality thereafter. The Gini coefficient has remained fairly high since 1970, with the ratios generally moving in the range of 0.452 to 0.529. Indeed the Gini ratio worsened from 0.452 in 1999 to 0.462 in 2004. This is also supported by Table 2.5, which indicates that the share of the income levels of the bottom 40 percent households declined from 14.5 percent in 1990 to 13.5 percent in 2004 while the share of the income levels of the top 20 percent increased slightly from 50 percent in 1990 to 51.2 percent

Table 2.4 Incidence of Poverty and Income Inequality

Year	Overall	Rural	Urban	Malay	Chinese	Indian	Hard-core poor	Household income distribution Gini coefficient
1970	52.4	58.7	21.3	65.9	27.5	40.2	–	0.506
1976	42.4	50.9	18.7	56.4	19.2	28.5	–	0.529
1980	29.2	37.4	12.6	–	–	–	–	0.493
1984	20.7	27.3	8.5	25.8	7.8	10.1	–	0.474
1987	17.3	22.4	8.1	23.8	7.1	9.7	–	0.458
1990	16.5	21.8	7.5	20.8	5.7	8.0	3.9	–
1993	13.5	18.6	5.3	–	–	–	–	0.459
1995	8.7	15.3	3.7	12.2	2.1	2.6	–	0.464
1997	6.8	11.8	2.4	–	–	–	1.4	0.47
1999	8.1	12.4	3.4	–	2.6	1.9	1.4	0.452
2000	5.5	10	1.9	–	–	–	–	–
2002	5.1	11.4	2.0	7.3	1.5	1.9	1.0	0.461
2004	5.7	11.9	2.5	8.3	0.6	2.9	1.2	0.462
2007	3.6	7.1	2.0	5.1	0.6	2.5	0.7	0.441
2009	3.8	8.4	1.7	5.3	0.6	2.5	–	0.441
2012	1.7	3.4	1.0	2.2	0.3	1.8	0.2	0.431
2014	0.6	1.6	0.3	0.8	0.1	0.6	0.1	0.401
2016	0.4	1.0	0.2	0.5	0.1	0.1	–	0.399

Source: Malaysia Economic Report (various years), Malaysia Five Years Plans (Seventh, Eighth, Ninth, e.g., Ninth Malaysia Plan-Table 16.3, p. 333), Anoma Abhayaratne (2003), Ministry of Economic Affairs, Malaysia.

Table 2.5 Income Shares by Income Group and Location

	1970	1973	1976	1984	1987	1990	1995	1997	1999	2004	2007	2009	2012	2014	2016
Total															
Top 20 Pct	55.9	53.7	61.9	53.2	51.2	50.0	51.3	52.4	50.5	51.2	49.8	49.6	48.6	46.6	46.2
Middle 40 Pct	32.5	34.0	27.8	34.0	35.0	35.5	35.0	34.4	35.5	35.3	35.6	36.1	36.6	36.9	37.4
Bottom 40 Pct	11.6	12.3	10.3	12.8	13.8	14.5	13.7	13.2	14.0	13.5	14.6	14.3	14.8	16.5	16.4
Urban															
Top 20 Pct	55	–	–	52.1	50.8	–	49.8	50.2	48.9	49.8	48.6	48.2	47.5	45.9	45.4
Middle 40 Pct	32.8	–	–	34.5	35.0	–	35.7	35.6	36.7	35.6	36.2	36.5	36.9	36.9	37.6
Bottom 40 Pct	12.2	–	–	13.4	14.3	–	14.5	14.2	14.9	14.6	15.2	15.3	15.6	17.1	17.0
Rural															
Top 20 Pct	51	–	–	49.5	48.3	–	47.4	48.2	48.0	46.0	45.7	47.4	44.8	42.7	43.4
Middle 40 Pct	35.9	–	–	36.4	36.7	–	37.1	36.6	36.7	37.4	36.9	36.4	38.0	38.9	38.5
Bottom 40 Pct	13.1	–	–	14.1	15.0	–	15.5	15.2	15.6	16.6	17.4	16.2	17.1	18.4	18.1

Source: Malaysia First, Second and Third Outline Perspective Plans. For example, Table 4.1, p. 89 in the Third Outline Perspective Plan, Ministry of Economic Affairs, Malaysia.

in 2004. The share of the income levels of the bottom 40 percent was the lowest ranging between 10.3 percent and 14.5 percent for the 1970 to 2004 period, while the share of the income levels of the top 20 percent was the highest ranging between 50 percent and 61.9 percent. Meanwhile, the share of the income levels of the middle 40 percent ranged between 27.8 percent and 35.5 percent. The Gini coefficients, nevertheless, began to decline in 2007 and reached 0.399 in 2016. Instead, having revised the country's poverty line (PLIs) in July 2020, there is still 5.6 percent of the population living in absolute poverty. The poverty rate remains higher than it should be – a reflection of the growth of income inequality that has contributed to widespread perceptions of the poor and vulnerable being left behind. And now, the government tends to focus more targeted measures on addressing the well-being of the poor and the vulnerable group.

While the overall income inequality seemed to have enhanced over the period, as reflected by the Gini coefficients, the disparity of incomes among the different income groups remained a challenge in practice. Overall, the bottom 40 percent registered a rising share – increasing from only 13.5 percent in 2004 to 16.4 percent in 2016 despite a low decreased rate for the top 20 percent (reduced gradually from the peak of 51.2 percent in 2004 to 46.2 percent in 2016). In the meantime, the share of the middle 40 percent ranged between 35.3 percent and 37.4 percent during the period. On top of that, trends in the series for urban and rural areas broadly followed the aggregate income inequality picture, with the rural income figure lower than that of the urban. Separately, the share of the bottom 40 percent of 18.1 percent of the rural areas was high compared to the share of 17.0 percent of the urban areas. The urban areas had a large share of the top 20 percent of 45.4 percent compared to 43.4 percent of the rural areas.

The incidence of poverty in the rural areas was about two times of that in the urban areas, a relativity which had remained broadly constant since the 1970s. Urban–rural disparities rose in the 1990s and had started to drop since 2004. Table 2.6 indicates that the income disparity between the urban and rural households deteriorated from 1:1.81 in 1999 to 1:2.11 in 2004 but improved later. 1:1.76 was recorded in 2016.

Among the ethnic groups, the Malays who mostly lived in rural areas were known as poor. The ethnic groups and regional discrepancies contributed much by the fact that the small-scale agricultural activities in the rural areas were mainly undertaken by the Malays, where per capita income was the lowest among all sectors, whereas the manufacturing and services industries in and near urban areas were largely owned and managed by non-Malays, particularly the Chinese where per capita income was much higher than in agriculture. Table 2.6 indicates that the income of the Chinese was more than two times the income of the Malays and the income of the Indians was

Table 2.6 Peninsular Malaysia: Mean Monthly Household Incomes by Ethnic Group and Stratum 1970–2004

	All	Malay (M)	Chinese (C)	Indian (I)	Others	Urban (U)	Rural (R)	C/M	I/M	U/R
1970	423	276	632	478	1,304	687	321	2.3	1.73	2.14
1973	502	335	739	565	1,798	789	374	2.21	1.69	2.11
1976	566	380	866	592	1,395	913	431	2.28	1.56	2.12
1979	669	475	906	730	1,816	942	531	1.91	1.54	1.77
1984	792	616	1,086	791	1,775	1,114	596	1.76	1.28	1.87
1987	760	614	1,012	771	2,043	1,039	604	1.65	1.26	1.72
1990	1,167	940	1,631	1,209	955	1,617	951	1.74	1.29	1.7
1992	1,563	–	–	–	–	–	–	1.73	1.26	1.75
1995	2,020	1,604	2,890	2,140	1,284	2,589	1,326	1.8	1.33	1.95
1997	2,606	–	–	–	–	3,357	1,704	1.83	1.42	2.04
1999	2,472	1,984	3,456	2,702	1,371	3,103	1,718	1.74	1.36	1.81
2002	3,011	2,376	4,279	3,044	2,165	3,652	1,729	1.8	1.28	2.1
2004	3,022	2,522	4,127	3,215	2,150	3,680	1,744	1.64	1.27	2.11
2007	3,686	3,156	4,853	3,799	3,561	4,356	2,283	1.54	1.20	1.91
2009	4,025	3,624	5,011	3,999	3,640	4,705	2,545	1.38	1.10	1.85
2012	5,000	4,457	6,366	5,233	3,843	5,742	3,080	1.43	1.17	1.86
2014	6,141	5,548	7,666	6,246	6,011	6,833	3,831	1.38	1.13	1.78
2016	6,958	6,267	8,750	7,150	4,951	7,671	4,359	1.40	1.14	1.76

Source: Jomo (2006), Malaysia Five Year Plans (Seventh, Eighth, Ninth, example: Ninth Malaysia Plan–Table 16.3, p. 333), Malaysia Economic Report (various years), Ministry of Economic Affairs, Malaysia.

more than one and half times the income of the Malays during the 1970s. Generally, the income disparities between the Malays and the Chinese and the Malays and the Indians improved throughout the 1970 to 2016 period. However, the income disparity ratio was still high where the income of the Chinese was around one and half times the income of the Malays and the income of the Indians was more than one time the income of the Malays during the 2000s and the 2010s.

All ethnic groups recorded a significant deterioration in the intra-ethnic Gini coefficient from 1999 to 2004 with a particularly high incidence of poverty in urban areas, as shown in Table 2.7. Inequality among the Malays was the highest compared with the Chinese and the Indians. The Gini coefficient among the Malays, which was 0.433 in 1999 increased to 0.452 in 2004, while the Gini coefficient among the Chinese and the Indians increased, from 0.434 and 0.413 in 1999 to 0.446 and 0.425 in 2004, respectively. Yet, the intra-ethnic Gini coefficients declined thereafter. In other words, on the average inequality improved in all the major ethnic groups from 2004 to 2016. For instance, inequality among the Chinese improved to the Gini coefficient of 0.411 in 2016 from 0.446 in 2004 and 0.425 in 2009, although it was still the highest in contrast to 0.385 and 0.382 for the Malays and the Indians, respectively.

However, throughout the NEP, Malay incomes gained relative to the incomes of both the Chinese and the Indian communities. But the former still remained significantly lower than the latter two. This is shown by the ownership of share capital. The proportion of Bumiputera equity ownership increased dramatically from 2.4 percent in 1970 to 20.6 percent in 1995, and then declined slightly to 18.9 percent in 2000 (Roslan, 2001). According to the Ninth Malaysia Plan, the proportion of Bumiputera equity ownership remained at 18.9 percent and the share capital of the Chinese was more than double that of the Bumiputera at 39 percent, while the share

Table 2.7 Gini Coefficient by Ethnic Group and Strata 1999, 2004, 2009 and 2016

	1999	2004	2009	2016
Malay	0.433	0.452	0.44	0.385
Chinese	0.434	0.446	0.425	0.411
Indian	0.413	0.425	0.424	0.382
Others	0.393	0.462	0.495	0.391
Malaysia	**0.452**	**0.462**	**0.441**	**0.399**
Urban	0.432	0.444	0.423	0.389
Rural	0.421	0.397	0.407	0.364

Source: Ninth Malaysia Plan, Ministry of Economic Affairs, Malaysia.

Table 2.8 Ownership of Share Capital of Limited Companies by Ethnic Group
2004, 2006 and 2008

Ownership group	2004	2006	2008
Bumiputera	18.9	19.4	21.9
Non-Bumiputera (Chinese, Indian and Others)	40.6	43.9	36.7
Chinese	39.0	42.4	34.9
Indian	1.2	1.1	1.6
Others	0.4	0.4	0.1
Nominee companies	8.0	6.6	3.5
Foreigners	32.5	30.1	37.9
Total*	100.0	100.0	100.0

Source: Tenth Malaysia Plan, p. 425.

Note: * The total for Bumiputera, non-Bumiputera, nominee companies and foreigners.
The information is publicly available only up to 2008.

of equity ownership held by the Indians and foreigners was 1.2 percent
and 32.5 percent, respectively (National Printing Department, 2006). Bumiputera ownership of share capital at par value increased from RM63 billion
in 2000 to RM100 billion in 2004. It rose marginally to RM127 billion compared to the non-Bumiputera at 36.7 percent in 2008. The achievement of
the Bumiputera at 21.9 percent in 2008 still fell short of the NEP target of
30 percent in spite of the emphasis on corporate equity allocation directly
to the Bumiputera in the past.

The government policies were considered to have achieved the restructuring of employment targets. Total employment increased from 3.4 million
in 1970 to 8.5 million in 2000 and to 14.8 million in 2018. Consistent with
the increase in employment, unemployment decreased from 7.8 percent in
1970 to 3.4 percent in 2000 and to 3.3 percent in 2018. Table 2.9 shows
that the percentage of Bumiputera in professional and technical occupations
increased and so did the percentage of Bumiputera in all other occupations. The percentage of Bumiputera in professional and technical categories increased from 47.0 percent in 1970 to 58.5 percent in 2000 and to
65.4 percent in 2018. However, the Bumiputera employment share in the
agricultural sector was still high rising from 72 percent in 1970 to 77.1 percent in 2000 and to 86.3 percent in 2018. In addition, the percentage of
Bumiputera in positions of senior officers and managers that was previously maintained at below 40 percent, increased slightly from 36.6 percent
in 2000 to 37.1 percent in 2005, and increased to 44.2 percent in 2018. The
percentage of Chinese as senior officers and managers was the highest at
55.1 percent in 2005 and had a slight decrease to 48.3 percent in 2018. For
example the percentage of Bumiputera chief executive officers (CEOs) was
20 percent compared to 70.4 percent of the Chinese in 2005.

Table 2.9 Employment by Ethnic Group and Occupation (Pct of Total)

Occupation	1970				1985				2000				2005				2018			
	B	C	I		B	C	I	O	B	C	I	O	B	C	I	O	B	C	I	O
Senior officer & managers	24.1	62.9	7.8		28.2	66.0	5.0	0.8	36.6	55.8	6.6	0.9	37.1	55.1	7.1	0.7	44.2	48.3	7.1	0.4
Professionals & technical	47.0	39.5	10.8		54.4	32.4	11.1	2.1	58.5	31.9	8.7	1.0	59.0	30.8	9.1	1.1	65.4	26.8	7.3	0.5
Clerical	35.4	45.9	17.2		54	36.8	8.7	0.5	56.6	35.4	7.4	0.5	56.7	34.3	8.4	0.5	60.2	31.8	7.2	0.8
Services & sales	35.5	50.7	12.9		47.9	44	7.5	0.65	51.2	40.6	7.3	0.9	51.5	39.6	8	0.9	66.6	27.7	4.7	1.0
Agricultural	72	18.3	9.7		73.5	17.2	8.3	1.1	77.1	13.9	5.5	3.6	80.8	11.3	4.3	3.7	86.3	11.1	1.8	1.0
Production	34.2	55.9	9.6		45.5	43.1	10.9	0.5	52	32.7	12.1	3.2	53.6	31.5	11.9	2.9	68.2	20.7	10.0	1.1

Source: Ninth Malaysia Plan – Table 16.4, p. 334, Anoma Abhayaratne (2003), Ministry of Economic Affairs, Malaysia.

Notes: B = Bumiputera, C = Chinese, I = Indian, O = Others.

It shows clearly that income inequality was still an important matter for Malaysia. It was likely that less government interventions for redistribution that began in the late 1980s had contributed to an overall increase as well as to the rural–urban and inter-ethnic income inequality since the 1990s.

In relation to this, the government undertook a more active role in the Ninth Malaysia Plan to reduce income inequality. The government targeted to narrow the income gap between the Malays and the Chinese from 1:1.64 in 2004 to 1:1.50 in 2010 and between the Malays and the Indians from 1:1.27 in 2004 to 1:1.15 in 2010. -Moreover, the government also targeted to reduce the rural–urban gap from 1:2.11 in 2004 to 1:2.0 in 2010. In relation to the Bumiputera equity ownership, the target was to attain between 20 and 25 percent by 2010 in order to reach the ultimate target of at least 30 percent by 2020. The incidence of poverty was to be reduced to 2.8 percent and hardcore poverty was to be completely eliminated by 2010.

The Tenth Malaysia Plan and the Eleventh Malaysia plan were oriented toward the low-income groups and the vulnerable with specific needs, regardless of race and location. The government intended to decrease the incidence of poverty from 3.8 percent in 2009 to 2 percent in 2015, while the Gini coefficient would be reduced from 0.441 to 0.420 to enhance overall income inequality. Then, income inequality was expected to improve further with the Gini coefficient being reduced to 0.385 in 2020. To elevate the livelihood of the income levels of the bottom 40 percent, the government aimed to double their mean incomes at the end of the 11MP, from RM1,440 in 2009 to RM2,537 in 2014. This would uplift the bottom 40 percent to the middle-income groups. Besides, the Bumiputera equity ownership was targeted not only to achieve at least 30 percent by 2020 but also to broaden Bumiputera participation in business.

Earlier discussion shows that the Malaysian economy exhibited a number of economic features, most of which were of special interest to macroeconomist modelers and development economists, which included persistence in rural–urban bias in the scope of inter-ethnic inequality. To account for this characteristic feature of the Malaysian economy, the urban and the rural sectors and household inter-ethnic differences remained an important aspect of the Malaysian SAM, which was going to be built in order to analyze the impact of public expenditure on income distribution in Malaysia.

2.6   General Structure and Trends in Public Sector Expenditure

Public expenditure can be broadly categorized into two categories; current and development expenditures. Current expenditure refers to the operating expenses required for the day-to-day functioning of the government departments. The current expenditure is mainly channeled to expenditure on emoluments, pensions and gratuities for different sectors, supplies and services (maintenance of facilities, buildings and infrastructure for different sectors), grants to state and debt service charges. Development expenditure refers to the creation or acquisition of fixed assets and sometimes is used to improve the existing facilities, and thus called capital expenditure.

Development expenditure reflects changes in policy focus and indicates the direction toward which the government is heading and thus will be given more emphasis in this chapter. Current expenditure nevertheless is not less important because expenditure on emoluments, pensions and gratuities is the main source of income for the government servant.

Throughout the 1966 to 2018 period, current expenditure formed a larger proportion of the total expenditure compared to development expenditure as indicated in Table 2.10. The share of the current expenditure was 76.9 percent during 1966–1970, 75.4 percent during 2006–2010 and achieved an all-time high amounting to 82.4 percent during 2016–2018

Table 2.10 Public Sector Expenditure

(Pct)	1966–1970	1971–1975	1976–1980	1981–1985	1986–1990	1991–1995	1996–2000	2001–2005	2006–2010	2011–2015	2016–2018
Current expenditure of total expenditure	76.9	70.8	65.5	63	75.8	75.1	70.9	69.6	75.4	82.0	82.4
Development expenditure of total expenditure	23.1	29.2	34.5	37	24.2	24.9	29.1	30.4	24.6	18.0	17.6
Growth rate of total expenditure	7.2	20.1	21.2	8.9	7.1	7.3	11	8.8	6.8	3.2	4.9
Growth rate of current expenditure	7.1	18.1	16.5	13.3	5.9	8	9.5	11.7	7.3	4.4	3.9
Growth rate of development expenditure	8.3	27.2	30.2	1.6	12.9	6.3	15	3.3	5.6	−1.7	9.6

Source: Calculation based on data from BNM Quarterly Bulletin (various issues), Malaysia Treasury Statistics from www.Treasury.gov.my

Notes: All figures are an average annual percentage during the period.
Public sector expenditure refers to federal government expenditure.

compared to the share of the development expenditure at 23.1 percent during 1966–1970, 24.6 percent during 2006–2010 and only 17.6 percent during 2016–2018.

For the 1966 to 1985 period, the share of current expenditure declined, while the share of development expenditure increased. The share of current expenditure declined from 76.9 percent during 1966–1970 to 63 percent during 1981–1985, while the share of development expenditure increased from 23.1 percent during 1966–1970 to 37 percent during 1981–1985. This was because current expenditure increased at a slower rate at an average rate of 13.7 percent per annum as compared to 16.9 percent per annum for the development expenditure. The higher growth rate of the development expenditure was due to the intensive implementation of the NEP. But after that period, the share of current expenditure increased from about 70 percent during 2001–2005 to 82.4 percent during 2016–2018, reaching a high record. A slight decrease of 65.3 percent happened during 2006–2008 (about the same level as during 1981–1985).

It is also interesting to note the growth rates of both expenditures during the economic crisis. The growth rate of the development expenditure was significantly lower relative to the current expenditure during the 1981–1985 period. Meanwhile, the 1997 crisis showed a different pattern where the growth rate of the development expenditure was relatively higher than the current expenditure during 1996–2000. Although the development planning underwent significant changes by placing equal weight to the role of both the government and private sectors, the growth rate of the development expenditure was still somewhat lower than the current expenditure during 2006–2010. This reflected that the government played more roles in economic recovery in the 1997 crisis as compared to the 1980s and the 2008 crises.

Another important thing to catch from the trend is that the scope for limiting or reducing the current expenditure was limited by the fact that a large proportion of the current expenditure was accounted by committed expenses comprising emoluments, pensions and gratuities, and debt service charges.

2.6.1   *Current Expenditure*

Table 2.11 in the functional classification of the current expenditure illustrates the trends and composition of the current expenditure from 1966 to 2018. Social services consistently formed the largest proportion of the current expenditure ranging from 27.8 percent to 39.3 percent of expenditure from 1966 to 2018. The other major components of current expenditure,

Table 2.11 Proportion of the Total Federal Government Current Expenditure: A Functional Classification

Pct	1966–1970	1971–1975	1976–1980	1981–1985	1986–1990	1991–1995	1996–2000	2001–2005	2006–2010	2011–2015	2016–2018
Defense and security	22.2	25.8	22.1	19	15.9	15.5	13.7	13.4	12.6	11.7	11.6
Economic services	5.2	5.6	6.2	9.2	8.3	9.2	9.7	8.3	9.2	9.1	8.1
Agriculture and rural development	2.7	2.5	3	4.7	4.2	3.7	2.7	2	2.7	2.3	2.0
Trade and industry	0.3	0.9	1.2	2.4	1.9	1.5	3.8	2.9	2.8	3.6	1.9
Public utilities	0	0	0	0	0.2	0.38	0.4	0.2	0.2	0.1	0.1
Transportation	1.9	1.6	1.2	1.5	1.7	3.4	2.5	2.9	3.4	2.6	2.8
Others[1]	0.3	0.6	0.8	0.6	0.27	0.98	0.27	0.26	0.1	0.5	1.4
Social services	35.5	35.6	34.8	27.8	27.9	31.2	34.1	35.7	36.8	36.4	39.3
Education	22.4	24.1	23.5	18.7	19.2	22.2	23.6	23.9	24.5	23.2	24.6
Health	7.6	7.7	7.3	5.6	5.4	5.9	7.4	7.7	7.9	8.9	10.8
Housing	0	0	0	0	0.3	0.2	0.3	0.5	0.7	0.7	0.2
Others[2]	5.5	3.8	4	3.5	3	2.9	2.8	3.6	3.7	3.6	3.7
Public debt charges	8.5	11.8	15	22.4	28.1	21.4	15.7	13.4	9.8	10.1	12.8
General administration	14.9	10.2	9.7	8.9	10.9	11.7	12.9	11.7	10.8	8.3	6.7
Other expenditures[3]	13.7	11	12.2	12.7	8.1	11	13.9	17.5	20.8	24.4	21.5

Source: Calculation based on data from BNM Quarterly Bulletin (various issues), BNM Annual Report (various years), Malaysia Economic Report (various years), Malaysia Five Year Plan (various plans), Malaysia Treasury Statistics from www.Treasury.gov.my.

Notes: All figures are an average annual proportion during the period.
1 Mainly telecommunications.
2 Mainly welfare services, sports labor and local government.
3 Includes grants and transfer to state governments as well as public agencies and enterprises.

ranked in descending order, were expenditure on defense and security, general administration, public debt charges, other expenditure and economic services[5] prior to 2010. Other expenditure that included public grants and transfers turned out to be the second highest during the 2010s, with the expenditure on defense and security, public debt charges, economic services and general administration following closely behind.

Expenditure on education was the major component in the social service category ranging from 18.7 percent to 24.6 percent of the current expenditure from 1966 to 2018. This was followed by expenditure on health ranging from 5.4 percent to 10.8 percent and others (which included welfare services, sports, labor and local government) ranging from 2.8 percent to 5.5 percent. The trend of allocation for the social service category declined and achieved the lowest proportion of 18.7 percent of the current expenditure during the economic crisis of 1981–1985, but since then had increased continuously until 2018.

Allocations for defense and security had been declining from year to year from 22.2 percent of the current expenditure during 1966–1970 to 11.6 percent during 2006–2018. This reflected improved security in Malaysia. Meanwhile, allocation for general administration declined from 14.9 percent of the current expenditure during 1966–1970 to 8.9 percent during 1981–1985, and then increased to 12.9 percent during 1996–2000 but declined gradually to 6.7 percent during 2016–2018. The consistent decline in the allocation to general administration for the 1966 to 1985 period and the 2001 to 2018 period reflected that the government's continuous effort to trim the civil services to control the draining of its financial resources especially at a time when the country was reeling under the effects of the prolonged global recession.

Allocations for public debt charges showed noticeable rising trends over time. It happened during the 1966 to 1985 period in the first place with an indication of an increasing proportion of the current expenditure, whereby the proportion more than tripled from 8.5 percent during 1966–1970 to 28.1 percent during 1981–1985. Government borrowing as a source of funds to finance development programs, increased and became high due to the higher interest rate environment during that period. The public debt charges, however, decreased continuously after that to about 10 percent during 2006–2010 – a reflection of the higher revenue received by the public sector. With a dramatic decrease in petroleum tax receipts, the public debt charges rose back to 12.8 percent during 2011–2018.

2.6.2 Development Expenditure

The objective of the development expenditure was mainly to achieve growth and income equality, and therefore it reflected changes in the income distribution policy and indicated the direction toward which the government was heading. Hence, a detailed elaboration on the development expenditure in relation to the income distribution policy is necessary to get a clear picture of the impact of the public sector development expenditure on income distribution in Malaysia.

Development expenditure, also called capital or investment expenditure, represents the expenditure undertaken by the government to build its investments. These investments enhance the productive capacity of the economy through the provision of facilities, infrastructure and capital goods. The actual impact of these investments on the growth process is magnified by the crowding in impact on private investment.

Table 2.12 in the functional classification of development expenditure pictures the structure and trend of development expenditure from 1966 to 2018. Allocation to economic services formed the largest proportion of the development expenditure. This was followed by the allocation to social services, defense and security, and general administration.

The largest proportion of the development expenditure in the economic services was not surprising since this expenditure on the various economic sectors must necessarily be of a capital in nature. Furthermore, given the importance of the public sector to lead the growth and development

Table 2.12 Proportion of the Total Federal Government Development Expenditure: A Functional Classification

Pct	1966– 1970	1971– 1975	1976– 1980	1981– 1985	1986– 1990	1991– 1995	1996– 2000	2001– 2005	2006– 2010	2011– 2015	2016– 2018
Defense and security	21.1	14.1	15.8	14.5	7.9	21.9	12.2	13.3	10.9	10.5	10.9
Economic services	58.9	68.3	65.1	58.5	63.5	47.9	46.5	39.3	50.3	59.5	58.1
Agriculture and rural development	27.7	24.2	19.1	13.6	16.1	11.5	5.9	6	9.2	5.4	5.2
Trade and industry	6.8	18.2	14.4	13.4	14.8	8.1	11.9	9.4	11.2	13.9	10.8
Public utilities	5.8	4.2	8.1	9.8	11.1	6.7	7.8	3.7	7.0	10.2	6.2
Transportation	12.5	17.7	18	15.1	19.2	21.5	20.2	19.2	19.7	19.6	23.8
Others[2]	6.1	4	5.5	6.5	2.3	0.3	0.7	0.9	3.2	10.4	12.1
Social services	17.5	14.9	16	25.3	25.7	25.9	32.2	39.7	33.6	26.7	26.5
Education	7.9	9.9	8	10.1	15.8	13.9	17.8	23.4	19.1	14.6	12.2
Health	4.2	2.4	1.4	1.4	2.2	4.5	3.6	5.5	4.9	4.0	3.4
Housing	4.8	1.9	5.3	11.1	3.9	1.9	4.6	4.5	4.0	2.2	2.9
Social & community services	0.6	0.7	1.3	2.7	3.8	5.6	6.2	6.3	5.6	5.9	7.8
General administration	2.5	2.7	3.1	1.7	2.9	4.3	9.1	7.7	5.2	3.3	4.6

Source: Calculation based on data from BNM Quarterly Bulletin (various issues), BNM Annual Report (various years), Malaysia Economic Report (various years), Malaysia Five Year Plan (various plans), Malaysia Treasury Statistics from www.Treasury.gov.my.

Notes: All figures are an average annual proportion during the period.
Table is reproduced from Table 1.3.

through public investment in various sectors, the expenditure could be expected to be substantial. This expenditure, however, showed a significant decreasing trend for the 1971 to 2005 period, from the highest 68.3 percent of the development expenditure during 1971–1975 to 39.3 percent during 2001–2005. The expenditure then rose back and was maintained at about 59 percent during 2011–2018.

The high proportion after the independence and particularly during the 1970s reflects the full involvement of the public sector in the NEP to achieve the two objectives: to eradicate poverty and to restructure the society. This was to solve the socio-economic imbalances that characterized the Malaysian society at that time. Emphasis was given to expenditure programs, which would have the greatest impact in reducing the wide economic and social imbalances within and among the ethnic groups and regions. In the 1980s, the government's continuous efforts to achieve these two NEP objectives could be seen from the continuous high proportion of the development expenditure in the economic sector. In the 1990s, however, there was a significant reduction in the proportion of the development expenditure in the economic services to below 50 percent until it achieved the lowest 39.3 percent during 2000–2005. This trend could reflect the decreasing involvement of the public sector in income distribution and the decreasing role of public investment in boosting the aggregate demand in the economy.

Among the outlays for economic services, the allocation for agriculture and rural development formed the largest proportion of the development expenditure in the 1960s and the 1970s owing to the dominance of the low-income group in the agricultural sector in rural areas. Agricultural and rural development project financing dealt with large and complex infrastructures that required high capital expenditures in particular.

Among the expenditure programs that had been implemented to raise productivity and income in agricultural activities were financing to improve input and facilities in existing agricultural areas, financing new land development schemes and financing agricultural research to modernize as well as to commercialize the agricultural practice. The most significant financing was on the opening up of new land in the jungle to plant rubber and palm oil in large-scale estates. Besides commercializing the rubber and palm oil activities, the scheme could enable the development of new townships in the rural areas and more importantly this new land was for the poor who did not have land. These activities were undertaken by the Federal Land Development Activity (FELDA), the FELCRA and the RISDA.

A substantial amount of expenditure was also spent on *in situ* programs, which involved the improvement of existing agricultural land through rubber replanting and the improvement of drainage and irrigation facilities.

The development of the *in situ* programs particularly was handled by the Integrated Agricultural Development Projects (IADPs), the Regional Development Authorities (RDAs), FELCRA, RISDA and the Farmers Organization Authority. Allocation for agriculture and rural development, which formed the largest proportion at 27.7 percent of the development expenditure during 1966–1970, however, declined to reach only 6 percent during 2000–2005. The significant reduction of the development expenditure on agriculture and rural development supports the aforementioned ideas on the decrease in public sector involvement in the income distribution strategy as agriculture and the rural areas were closely associated with Malay low-income groups. At the same time it could reflect the decreasing importance of the agricultural sector in the economy.

In contrast, the transportation and the trade and industry sectors gradually accounted for a greater proportion of the outlays. They only accounted for 12.5 percent and 6.8 percent of the development expenditure respectively during 1966–1970, which rose to 19.6 percent and 13.9 percent during 2011–2015. Although the development expenditure for the trade and industry sectors showed a slight reduction during 2016–2018, the expenditure for transportation was at the highest proportion of the total development expenditure. The significant increase in the expenditure for transportation was initiated by the improvement and building of new roads and highways. Expenditure on transportation was important to provide an efficient system for supporting the private sectors as well as accelerating economic growth. Meanwhile, the increase in expenditure in the trade and industry sector was to accelerate industrial expansion, speed up the pace of regional development and increase Bumiputera participation in trade and industry. The increase also resulted from the rapid growth of small-scale industries mainly to encourage the Malays and the low-income people to be involved in business.

Development expenditure on public utilities was relatively low, less than or about 10 percent of the total development expenditure. Expenditure on utilities included investment on electricity, water supply and sewerage, and other utility projects. Other outlays on economic services were very low for the 1966–2010 period, but it dramatically increased to 10.4 percent during 2011–2015 and 12.1 percent during 2016–2018.

In framing the pattern of the government development expenditure in economic services, it seems that the government's main emphasis was given to projects which would increase productivity and investment in a wide range of industries. While maintaining this broad focus, emphasis was given to the importance of achieving a better distribution of income among the ethnic groups and regions in the country but at a lesser extent. Therefore, although there was substantial economic growth, economic imbalances still existed at a considerable degree.

Development expenditure for social services, which ranked second, increased from 17.5 percent during 1966–1970 to 33.6 percent during 2006–2010, and yet it gradually reduced and was maintained at around 26.5 percent during 2011–2018. The possibility is that such a change was mainly contributed through the continuous provision of a wide range of free or subsidized social and educational facilities. Allocation for education consistently increased from 7.9 percent of the development expenditure during 1966–1970 to 23.4 percent during 2001–2005 but constantly decreased to only 12.2 percent during 2016–2018. This expenditure was to provide appropriate educational and training programs and facilities to increase the supply of trained manpower. Similarly, allocation for social and community services consistently increased from 0.6 percent of the development expenditure during 1966–1970 to 6.3 percent during 2001–2005 and reached 7.8 percent during 2016–2018 after a slight decrease of 5.6 percent during 2006–2010. This trend reflected the efforts of the government to improve social elements along with economic elements to ensure a stable and sustainable economic growth. This also indicated the focus of the government on human resource development through training and education, not only as an engine of economic growth but also more importantly for the poor to come out from poverty.

Allocation for health services at first declined from 4.2 percent of the development expenditure during 1966–1970 to 1.4 percent during 1981–1985, but then increased to record 5.5 percent during 2001–2005 and then remained at modest levels through the following years. Improvement in health services would lead to a better quality of life through improvements to health conditions. Furthermore, improvement in health conditions will increase labor productivity by reducing the loss of working hours through illness.

Allocation to housing fluctuated ranging from 1.9 percent during 1971–1975 to the highest during the economic crisis of 1981–1985 at 11.1 percent. This expenditure was an important component of the development expenditure to eradicate poverty. The public sector housing programs involved the provision of housing for poor people in both the rural and urban areas. Free new housing was provided for the hard-core poor while low cost housing was provided for poor people. To accelerate the development of low cost housing, there were joint ventures between the public and the private sectors.

Development expenditure for defense and security was mainly for the purchase of military equipment, vehicles, accommodation and bases. The public sector cut the expenditure significantly to 7.9 percent of the development expenditure during 1986–1990, which was just after the economic crisis, as the government used the money for other expenditure for economic recovery purposes. After that the expenditure jumped up to 21.9 percent during 1991–1995 but declined since then to achieve 10.9 percent during 2016–2018.

Development expenditure for general administration also followed a similar trend where there was a significant cut in expenditure to 1.7 percent of the development expenditure during the economic crisis. However, overall development expenditure for general administration showed an increasing trend from 2.5 percent during 1966–1970 to 7.7 percent during 2001–2005 and remained roughly at 5 percent during 2016–2018. This expenditure was mainly to provide adequate physical facilities for a better working environment, which would lead to increased output and the quality of service, particularly the provision of office accommodation.

Indeed the pervasiveness in public expenditure gave greater significance to public finance as an instrument for mobilizing resources. This was the measure of using the fiscal system on the expenditure sides to capture resources for the purpose of development and to use them in top priority investment projects.

2.7 Budget Management

Table 2.13 shows the public sector budget management throughout the 1964 to 2018 period. The 1970s saw the public sector's important role in the economy as it took on a more direct and active role in the country's social and economic development process. This was reflected by the continuous deficit during this period from 3.91 percent of the GDP in 1970 to 7.16 percent in 1980. Public sector participation in the economy expanded further in the early 1980s as it pursued an expansionary countercyclical fiscal policy to ride out the effects of the global recession. The countercyclical policy led to a higher deficit in the government's fiscal position in 1981, 1982 and 1983, which recorded 16.1 percent, 17.36 percent and 10.55 percent of the GDP, respectively.

When confronted with this higher deficit problem, the government implemented comprehensive structural programs to reduce spending and reordered national objectives consistent with the domestic resource availability. Among the most significant new directions in the public policy was the promotion of the private sector as the main engine of growth. This resulted in the reduction of public sector commercial activities through the privatization program. The shift emphasized the private sector-driven growth's contributions, which led to a significant improvement in the government's financial position, a lower fiscal deficit position recorded during the late 1980s and even achieved a fiscal surplus for five years from 1993 to 1997.

Due to the Asian financial crisis in 1997, an expansionary countercyclical fiscal policy resulted in a fiscal deficit of 1.76 percent of the GDP in 1998, the

Table 2.13 Government Fiscal Accounts

Year	Current revenue	Current expenditure	Current surplus/ deficit	Development expenditure	Repayment	Overall surplus/ deficit	Current surplus/ GDP	Overall surplus/ GDP
	RM Million						*(Pct)*	
1964	1,469	1,387	82	422	79	−419	1.05	−5.36
1965	1,591	1,539	52	517	66	−531	0.61	−6.18
1966	1,667	1,620	47	547	96	−596	0.51	−6.49
1967	1,840	1,789	51	519	100	−568	0.53	−5.89
1968	1,891	1,799	92	496	112	−516	0.91	−5.12
1969	2,094	1,933	161	504	100	−443	1.47	−4.05
1970	2,400	2,163	237	725	13	−475	1.95	−3.91
1971	2,418	2,398	20	1,085	15	−1,050	0.16	−8.4
1972	2,920	3,068	−148	1,242	19	−1,371	−1.08	−10.05
1973	3,399	3,342	57	1,128	22	−1,049	0.33	−6.01
1974	4,791	4,318	473	1,878	24	−1,381	2.23	−6.5
1975	5,117	4,900	217	2,151	33	−1,901	1	−8.8
1976	6,157	5,528	629	2,378	44	−1,705	2.32	−6.29
1977	7,760	7,098	662	3,217	79	−2,476	2.13	−7.97
1978	8,841	7,391	1,450	3,782	83	−2,249	4.01	−6.22
1979	10,505	7,890	2,615	4,281	131	−1,535	5.89	−3.45
1980	13,926	10,292	3,534	7,470	132	−3,704	6.83	−7.16
1981	15,806	13,686	2,120	11,358	223	−9,015	3.79	−16.1
1982	16,690	15,922	768	11,485	296	−10,421	1.28	−17.36
1983	18,608	16,124	2,484	9,670	253	−6,933	3.78	−10.55
1984	20,805	17,506	3,299	8,407	333	−4,775	4.43	−6.42
1985	21,115	18,766	2,349	7,142	386	−4,407	3.03	−5.69
1986	19,518	20,075	−557	7,559	610	−7,506	−0.72	−9.7
1987	18,143	20,185	−2,042	4,741	630	−6,153	−2.56	−7.73
1988	21,967	21,212	755	5,231	1,186	−3,290	0.83	−3.62
1989	25,273	22,982	2,291	7,696	1,995	−3,410	2.23	−3.32
1990	29,251	25,026	4,495	10,689	2,757	−3,437	3.77	−2.89
1991	34,053	28,296	5,757	9,565	1,168	−2,640	4.26	−1.95
1992	39,250	3,2075	7,175	9,688	1,270	−1,243	4.76	−0.82
1993	41,691	32,217	9,474	10,124	1,004	354	5.5	0.21
1994	49,446	35,064	14,382	11,277	1,303	4,408	7.36	2.26
1995	50,954	36,573	14,381	14,051	1,531	1,861	6.46	0.84
1996	58,280	43,865	14,415	14,628	2,028	1,815	5.68	0.72
1997	65,736	44,665	21,071	15,750	1,305	6,626	7.48	2.35
1998	56,710	44,584	12,126	18,103	975	−5,002	4.26	−1.76
1999	58,675	46,699	11,976	22,614	1,152	−9,486	3.99	−3.16
2000	61,864	56,547	5,317	27,941	2,909	−19,715	1.55	−5.74

Year	Current revenue	Current expenditure	Current surplus/ deficit	Development expenditure	Repayment	Overall surplus/ deficit	Current surplus/ GDP	Overall surplus/ GDP
	RM Million						(Pct)	
2001	79,567	63,757	15,810	35,235	1,003	−18,422	4.73	−5.51
2002	83,515	68,699	14,816	35,977	908	−20,253	4.09	−5.59
2003	92,608	75,224	17,384	39,353	1,041	−20,928	4.4	−5.3
2004	39,397	91,298	8,099	28,864	13,64	−19,419	1.8	−4.31
2005	10,6304	97,744	8,560	30,534	3,250	−18,724	1.64	−3.58
2006	12,3546	107,694	15,852	35,807	846	−19,109	2.76	−3.33
2007	13,9885	123,084	16,801	40,564	3,105	−20,659	2.62	−3.22
2008	159,793	153,499	6,295	42,847	959	−35,594	0.98	−5.57
2009	158,639	157,067	1,573	49,515	519	−47,424	0.25	−7.53
2010	159,653	151,633	8,020	52,792	1,496	−43,275	0.98	−5.27
2011	185,419	182,593	2,826	46,416	1,082	−42,509	0.33	−4.91
2012	207,913	205,537	2,376	46,932	2,606	−41,950	0.26	−4.60
2013	213,370	211,270	2,100	42,210	1,526	−38,584	0.22	−4.04
2014	220,626	219,589	1,037	39,503	1,052	−37,414	0.10	−3.70
2015	219,089	216,998	2,091	40,768	1,483	−37,194	0.20	−3.50
2016	212,421	210,173	2,248	41,995	1,346	−38,401	0.20	−3.46
2017	220,406	217,695	2,711	44,884	1,852	−40,321	0.23	−3.43
2018	236,460	235,450	1,010	54,900	563	−53,327	0.08	−4.34

Source: BNM Quarterly Bulletin (various issues), Malaysia Economic Reports (various years), Malaysia Treasury Statistics from www.Treasury.gov.my

deficit that emerged again after five years of surpluses. As global economic uncertainties continued to persist, the 1999–2009 budgets maintained an expansionary stance. Hence, the fiscal deficit continued from 3.16 percent of the GDP in 1999 to 4.81 percent in 2008 and to 7.53 percent in 2009. The fiscal deficits were seen to be on a downward trajectory after the public finance reform initiatives such as the rationalization of subsidies and the adoption of Goods and Services Tax (GST) of 6 percent in 2015. The fiscal deficit slid to less than 4.5 percent in 2018.

Among the considerations taken to determine whether the size of the fiscal deficit was manageable were: the revenue was able to meet the operating expenditure and hence, a surplus in the current account was maintained at all times; the availability of domestic and external financing without crowding out the private sector, and the debt servicing was not very high.

Government revenue and domestic and external borrowing are the main sources for finance fiscal expansion. As indicated in Table 2.14, revenue receipts were enormously robust where the total revenue registered an

Table 2.14 Federal Government Revenue

Item	RM Million				Average annual growth rate	
	2000	2005	2008	2018	2000–2008	2008–2018
Total revenue	61,864	106,304	161,558	236,460	12.75	3.88
Taxes	47,173	80,594	107,737	174,700	10.88	4.95
Direct taxes	29,156	53,543	77,579	133,474	13.01	5.58
Company	13,905	26,381	33,325	70,536	11.54	7.79
Individual	7,015	8,649	14,593	34,800	9.59	9.08
Petroleum	6,010	14,566	24,511	16,845	19.21	−3.68
Other	2,227	3,947	5,150	11,293	11.05	8.17
Indirect taxes	18,017	27,051	30,158	41,226	6.65	3.18
Non-tax revenue	14,691	25,710	53,821	61,761	17.62	1.39

Source: BNM Quarterly Bulletin (various issues), Ministry of Economic Affairs, Malaysia from https://mea.gov.my

average annual growth of 12.75 percent throughout 2000 to 2008. Government taxes revenue, as a main contributor to the total revenue, registered an average annual growth of 10.88 percent throughout the period. The increase was attributed to the higher revenue collected from company tax, petroleum tax and indirect taxes (export duties and excise duties). In 2008 the revenue of RM161.6 billion accounted for about 25 percent of the GDP. Over the next ten years, the average annual growth rate was at only 3.88 percent. The major source of tax collections, especially petroleum tax, had the worst slump with a negative growth rate of 3.68 percent of the annual average throughout 2008 to 2018. Only RM16,845 million was collected in 2018 compared with RM24,511 million in 2008. In 2018, the revenue was roughly 20 percent of the GDP.

Higher revenue along with higher expenditure contained the overall fiscal deficit below 6 percent of the GDP throughout the 2000 to 2018 period. The government revenue continued to increase to RM261,814 million in 2019 and with the continued expansion of the public expenditure, it recorded a fiscal deficit of 3.7 percent of the GDP.[6] The higher revenue enabled the current surplus to be maintained all the time (current surplus was recorded for most of the years). Maintaining at least a surplus position in the current account over the course of the business cycle reduced the long-term risks for the country.

High national savings that of an average of 30 percent of the GNP from 1965 to 2018 became one of the sources of financial capital for the government. Table 2.15 indicates that net domestic borrowing was the main source of financing for the federal government development expenditure,

Table 2.15 Federal Government Source of Financing

	1966–1970	1971–1975	1976–1980	1981–1985	1986–1990	1991–1995	1996–2000	2001–2005	2006–2010	2011–2015	2016–2018
					Pct						
Government current surplus*	17.8	6.1	39.7	25.6	11.6	103.3	81.6	38.9	22.6	5.0	4.4
Net domestic borrowing	54.9	63.5	50.7	46.1	113.2	15.4	27.3	51.4	80.4	98.2	96.0
Net foreign borrowing	9	25	14.2	35.1	−28.9	−26.3	−0.2	3.8	−4.9	0.3	0.1
Special receipts	6.9	2.3	0.5	0.4	2.7	2.7	1.1	0	0	0	0
Use of assets	11.4	3.1	−5.1	−7.2	1.4	4.9	−9.8	5.8	1.9	−3.6	−0.5
Total	100	100	100	100	100	100	100	100	100	100	100

Source: Calculation based on data from BNM Quarterly Bulletin (various issues), Malaysia Economic Report 2008/2009, Malaysia Treasury Statistics from www.treasury.gov.my

Note: * Government current surplus = Revenue – current expenditure.

which was recorded at over 50 percent from 1966 to 2018 except for the 1991–1995 and the 1996–2000 periods (during these periods, the current surplus was the main source of financing). Net domestic borrowing even achieved the highest, over 100 percent during 1986–1990 and stayed at nearly 100 percent over the 2011 to 2018 period. The bulk of the domestic borrowing was through the issuance of Malaysian Government Securities (MGS) to non-bank sources such as the Employees Provident Fund (EPF), other provident and pension funds and insurance companies.

Meanwhile, the proportion of net foreign borrowing for development expenditure was very low with less than 0.5 percent during 2011–2018 and was even recorded negative during 1991–1995, 1996–2000 and 2006–2010. The debt service ratio for external financing was low. As the bulk of the government borrowing was from MGS, which were non-inflationary sources, the government's exposure to exchange rate risks was kept low. Given that the MGS were raised at fixed interest rates, the exposure to interest rate changes was also low. In addition, as most of the debt had a long-term maturity, it was adequately spaced out to minimize the risks from bunching.

The fiscal stance indicated a policy deficit induced by the countercyclical measures taken by the government, and not induced by long-term structural rigidities arising from either the persistent decline in revenue or a locked-in operating expenditure due to inefficiency or weak fundamentals. Hence, the fiscal deficit was expected to be only transitory. In addition, the overall deficit due to higher development expenditure and not by the operating expenditure indicated that the capacity to move toward a surplus was greater when economic activities recovered.

More importantly, the fiscal expansion had not created structural imbalances in the economy. The government expenditure expansion had not resulted in higher inflation due to the excess capacity in the economy. Expenditure expansion did not result in leakages or put a strain in the balance of payments as most of the expenditure was on projects with minimal imports content. Projects selected under the expansion programs were those with strong linkages to the economy like education and training where these projects did not only stimulate economic growth in the new term but also helped to enhance the long-term objective of raising productivity. As most of the sources of financing were based on fixed interest rates, it enabled to contain the inflation rate. Furthermore, sufficient liquidity in the banking system to meet the private sector's financing needs also prevented any crowding out.

2.8   Conclusions

This chapter brought an understanding of the background of the country's economy by taking the income distribution analysis into consideration. The structure and trend in public sector expenditure were in need of revision to trace the restricted scope for national expenditure programs. The development and performance of the economy and society were first reviewed to depict the present state of the country. Attention was then drawn to the policy measures taken to curb poverty and income distribution and its trend related to poverty, incomes, shared capital and employment throughout the period. The composition of public expenditure was also in focus with particular emphasis on the current and the development expenditure. Moreover, the assessment of the direction of change of public revenues and expenditure would give an overview of the policy focus change being undertaken.

Malaysia has shown very courageous achievements in curbing economic hardships without leaving the people's quality of life behind. High dependence on trade usually exposes the country to be more vulnerable to the global impact. Still, the economy could have bounced back to growth from the deepest downturns on global markets over the decades. Nevertheless, poverty and income distribution have often been a central concern of the national development policies, especially a country with a multiracial population. Visionary policies such as the NEP, the NDP, Vision 2020 and the NTP included ideas of economic growth with zero poverty and income equality. The overall incidence of poverty has steadily been falling since the 1970s. The disparity of incomes, nevertheless, remained high. Also, the enhancement of income equality among the different ethnic groups was getting better and better. The urban–rural income gap, nevertheless, remained high where urban residents had notably higher incomes than the rural residents, while the country saw a growth in employment.

Despite this, the composition of public expenditure was in favor of the current expenditure where social services stood for the highest proportion from 1966 to 2018 consistently, while the largest share of the development expenditure went to the economic activities. Specifically, public expenditure on education received a high portion of the total social welfare expenditure. Besides, the dominance of the low-income group in the agricultural sector in the rural areas led to a large allocation of the development expenditure to be directed to agriculture and rural development during the 1960s and the 1970s. Nowadays, the transportation, and trade and industry sectors are increasingly counting on a greater proportion of the outlays. The development expenditure, classed as public capital or investment expenditure, showed distinct rising trends, in particular during a recession, in contrast to the current expenditure that covered the day-to-day operations of the government departments which grew in low rates.

The direct and active role the government played in the country's social and economic development process turned into a continuous deficit during this period. Besides, most of the domestic borrowing came from the issuance of Malaysian Government Securities (MGS) to support public finance, and the public finance reform initiatives such as the rationalization of subsidies came into place to confront the high deficit problem.

Notes

1 Bumiputera is an official definition that is widely used in Malaysia, embracing the Malays as well as other indigenous ethnic groups. The concept of a Bumiputera in Malaysia was coined by Tunku Abdul Rahman, the First Prime Minister of Malaysia, and has its roots in the recognition of the 'special position' of the Malays given by the Federal Constitution of Malaysia, in particular Article 153.

2 These NKEAs that included (1) the Greater Kuala Lumpur/Klang Valley; (2) oil, gas and energy; (3) financial services; (4) wholesale and retail; (5) palm oil and rubber; (6) tourism; (7) electrical and electronics; (8) business services; (9) communications content and infrastructure; (10) education; (11) agriculture and (12) healthcare were identified as high potential areas for economic leverage.

3 The NKRAS initially covered six priority areas and aligned in response to people's wants and needs. They were (1) reducing crime; (2) fighting corruption; (3) improving student outcomes; (4) raising living standards of low-income households; (5) improving rural basic infrastructure and (6) improving urban public transport. Addressing the cost of living was added afterward with the rising concern about the high cost of living due to inflation.

4 In 2009, the income levels of the bottom 40 percent covered a sum of 2.4 million households that evenly spread across rural and urban areas. 1.8 percent of them were within the hardcore poor group in this category, 7.6 percent within the poor group and the remaining 90.6 percent within the low-income households group. Indeed, the Bumiputera stood at about 73 percent.

5 This component of the current expenditure is classified by the functions and if
   the component of expenditure is classified by the object, it would appear that the
   payment of emoluments forms the largest component of the current expenditure.
6 The calculation was made on the basis of the figures from the official page of the
   Ministry of Economic Affairs, Malaysia.

References

Anoma Abhayaratne. (2003). *Poverty reduction strategies in Malaysia 1970–2000: Some
   lessons*. Sri Lanka: University of Peradeniya.
Malaysia. (1970). *Bank Negara Malaysia quarterly bulletin, 4, 1970*. Kuala Lumpur: Min-
   istry of Finance.
Malaysia. (1971). *Second Malaysia plan 1971–75*. Kuala Lumpur: National Printing
   Department.
Malaysia. (1972). *Bank Negara Malaysia quarterly bulletin, 4, 1972*. Kuala Lumpur: Min-
   istry of Finance.
Malaysia. (1975a). *Bank Negara Malaysia quarterly bulletin, 3, 1975*. Kuala Lumpur:
   Ministry of Finance.
Malaysia. (1975b). *Bank Negara Malaysia quarterly bulletin, 4, 1979*. Kuala Lumpur:
   Ministry of Finance.
Malaysia. (1976). *Third Malaysia plan 1976–1980*. Kuala Lumpur: National Printing
   Department.
Malaysia. (1981). *Fourth Malaysia plan 1981–1985*. Kuala Lumpur: National Printing
   Department.
Malaysia. (1982). *Bank Negara Malaysia quarterly bulletin, 3, 1982*. Kuala Lumpur: Min-
   istry of Finance.
Malaysia. (1985). *Bank Negara Malaysia quarterly bulletin, 3, 1985*. Kuala Lumpur: Min-
   istry of Finance.
Malaysia. (1986). *Fifth Malaysia plan 1986–1990*. Kuala Lumpur: National Printing
   Department.
Malaysia. (1991). *Sixth Malaysia plan 1991–95*. Kuala Lumpur: National Printing
   Department.
Malaysia. (1996a). *Economic report 1995/96*. Kuala Lumpur: Treasury Malaysia.
Malaysia. (1996b). *Seventh Malaysia plan 1996–2000*. Kuala Lumpur: National Print-
   ing Department.
Malaysia. (1999a). *Bank Negara Malaysia quarterly bulletin, 1, 1999*. Kuala Lumpur:
   Ministry of Finance.
Malaysia. (1999b). *Economic report 1998/99*. Kuala Lumpur: Treasury Malaysia.
Malaysia. (2000). *Bank Negara Malaysia annual report, 1999*. Kuala Lumpur: Ministry
   of Finance.
Malaysia. (2001a). *Bank Negara Malaysia annual report, 2000*. Kuala Lumpur: Ministry
   of Finance.
Malaysia. (2001b). *Economic report 2000/2001*. Kuala Lumpur: Treasury Malaysia
Malaysia. (2001c). *Eight Malaysia plan 2001–2005*. Kuala Lumpur: National Printing
   Department.
Malaysia. (2002). *Economic report 2001/2002*. Kuala Lumpur: Treasury Malaysia.

Malaysia. (2003). *Bank Negara Malaysia quarterly bulletin, 1, 2003*. Kuala Lumpur: Ministry of Finance.

Malaysia. (2005a). *Annual national product and expenditure accounts 1987–2004*. Kuala Lumpur: Department of statistics.

Malaysia. (2005b). *Bank Negara Malaysia quarterly bulletin, 1, 2005*. Kuala Lumpur: Ministry of Finance.

Malaysia. (2005c). *Economic report 2004/2005*. Kuala Lumpur: Treasury Malaysia.

Malaysia. (2005d). *Final national account statistics 2000*. Kuala Lumpur: Department of Statistics.

Malaysia. (2006a). *Bank Negara Malaysia quarterly bulletin, 4, 2006*. Kuala Lumpur: Ministry of Finance.

Malaysia. (2006b). *Economic report 2005/2006*. Kuala Lumpur: Treasury Malaysia.

Malaysia. (2007). *Economic report 2006/2007*. Kuala Lumpur: Treasury Malaysia.

Malaysia. (2008). *Economic report 2007/08*. Kuala Lumpur: Treasury Malaysia.

Malaysia. (2009a). *Bank Negara Malaysia quarterly bulletin, 1, 2009*. Kuala Lumpur: Ministry of Finance.

Malaysia. (2009b). *Economic report 2008/2009*. Kuala Lumpur: Treasury Malaysia.

Malaysia. (2010). *Tenth Malaysia plan 2011–2015*. Kuala Lumpur: National Printing Department.

Malaysia. (2015). *Eleventh Malaysia plan 2016–2020*. Kuala Lumpur: National Printing Department.

Malaysia. *Economic transformation programme*. Kuala Lumpur: Prime Minister's Department.

Malaysia. *Government transformation programme*. Kuala Lumpur: Prime Minister's Department.

Malaysia. *National transformation programme*. Kuala Lumpur: Prime Minister's Department.

Malaysia. *New economic model (2010–2020)*. Kuala Lumpur: National Economic Advisory Council.

Malaysia. *Statistic report*, from the Malaysia Treasury Department. Retrieved from www.treasury.gov.my

National Printing Department. (2006). *Ninth Malaysia Plan 2006–2010*.

3 Social Accounting Matrix as a Framework to Analyze the Impact of Public Expenditure on Income Distribution

3.1 Introduction

The SAM is a particular representation of the macro- and microeconomic accounts of a socio-economic system, which captures the transactions and transfers between all economic agents in the system (Roland-Host & Sancho, 1995; Pyatt, 1991; Pyatt & Round, 1977, 1979).

SAM presents data in the square matrix format and involves various sets of accounts, which represent the whole production and the institutional sectors of a given economy. Hence, it presents data in a relatively efficient way. It summarizes the interdependence between productive activities, factor shares, household income distribution, balance of payments and capital accounts for the economy as a whole at a point in time. Each account consists of a row for the recording of the incomes and a column for the recording of expenses. For a clear presentation, the sequence number of an account in the matrix is the same by row and by column.

This book constructs a structure of SAM for Malaysia focusing on the distribution of income among the ethnic groups across regions (rural–urban). The incorporation of different classes of public expenditure in SAM, then, is to analyze the impact of the public expenditure policy on income distribution in Malaysia. Hence, the structure of SAM will present the initial conditions which prevail in the economy and can trace the channel through which the public expenditure affects various segments in the economy, particularly the poor.

In SAM, a household really represents all the people in the society. It is important to consider the household as an institutional unit in SAM. Households are often considered to be behaviorally distinct units that make economic decisions about the supply of labor and consumption expenditure. Furthermore, definitions of poverty or economic welfare are often expressed in terms of per-capita household income and consumption. The household thus becomes the natural focus of SAM analysis.

DOI: 10.4324/9781003302506-3

The traditional approach assumes that public sector expenditure in the production sectors ultimately somehow benefits the household sector. Therefore, the public sector plays an important role in the redistribution process. The remaining part of the chapter is as follows: Section 3.2 presents the application of the SAM approach in empirical works in Malaysia. The detailed SAM modeling framework is discussed in Section 3.3 (on an aggregate basis), Section 3.4 (on a disaggregate basis) and Section 3.5 (on a functional basis). Section 3.6 elaborates policy experiments of the study and Section 3.7 includes the concluding remarks for the chapter.

3.2   SAM Application in Malaysia

The SAM framework had a relatively short history in Malaysia. Among the pioneers of SAM in Malaysia was by Ramesh, Gnasegarah, Pyatt, and Round (1980) where the distribution of income in the Malaysian economy in 1970 was examined. At about the same time, the equilibrium model was introduced by Ahluwia and Lysy (1979). The model, however, was mainly for theoretical issues and not meant for a serious empirical model for Malaysia. The model was a huge and complex structure. However, it was the pioneering model on Malaysia and the basis of the Economic Planning Unit (EPU) SAM model. In collaboration with EPU, World Bank experts, Pyatt, Round and Denes, constructed a national SAM for the Malaysian economy in 1970, which distinguished between Peninsular Malaysia (West) and the states of Sabah and Sarawak (East) in 1984. Zakariah (2005) further discussed the theoretical issues of the SAM applications in policy formulation in Malaysia.

Khor (1982), in doing his PhD study, used a dual approach in his SAM model to study income distribution and unemployment in Malaysia. He made an important distinction between the formal and informal sectors. The capitalist in the formal sector is assumed to maximize profits, while the one in the informal sector is assumed to maximize incomes. The model consists of 13 production industries: five labor types and three household groups. A more recent work was done by Saari, Dietzenbacher, and Los (2014) that looked at the sources of income inequality among the Malays, the Chinese, the Indians and the others (minorities such as Iban, Kadazan and Bajau) in Malaysia. These eight ethnic groups were further divided into high, medium and low education levels to explain workers' skills to accentuate differences in wage inequality for households. Their newly constructed SAM model for the year 2000 is a compilation of 134 accounts, which is made up primarily of 92 production industries, 27 labor categories and nine household groups (including foreigners).

It is important to note here that a significant limitation in all the previous Malaysian SAM and also many other SAM studies is that they merely focused on real economic activities or real accounts when studying income distribution without incorporating financial accounts. Though Ramesh et al. (1980) incorporated the domestic institution's capital accounts in their Malaysian SAM, it is in a consolidated form, no further disaggregation of the capital for separate institutions. Therefore, the principal loss in information contains saving investments or the flow of funds between institutions. Ramesh et al. (1980) state that 'to capture such detail for Malaysia, a good deal more work needs to be done and this might deserve a high priority in future developments' (p. 71).

Financial accounts capture the segmented nature of the saving-investment process of various institutions. An essential point is that larger aggregate savings today might not be able to generate a higher aggregate output tomorrow, but the pattern of savings and structural changes in the initial resource endowment may be more important determinants of future equity and growth. The pattern of savings are all including savings among household groups, enterprises and government institutions. It is not just the standard of living of the poor but also rather the amount of specific savings generated by them and the unfavorable initial resource endowment which they face. Therefore, the adoption of a financial account as a data system for multi-sectoral planning will incorporate these investment financing schemes in the framework, that is, households savings, government revenue surplus (taxes expenditures) and undistributed business profits (corporations savings).

Most of the studies in Malaysia are on the trend and determinants of income inequality. To our knowledge, none of the studies on relating public expenditure and income inequality were done in Malaysia. Moreover, most of the studies used other methods than SAM to analyze income distribution except Saari et al. (2014), Pyatt, Round, and Denes (1984), Khor (1982), Ramesh et al. (1980) and Ahluwia and Lysy (1979). Even though they used SAM in doing the analysis, their capital account in the SAM is in consolidated form.

This SAM was constructed to study public expenditure related to income distribution by improving the existing Malaysian SAM through the incorporation of disaggregating public capital investment and private capital investment according to different production sectors. The inclusion of the detailed composition of public sector capital investment in SAM has important potential to give a view on the role of the government as an intermediator among the sectors and the institutions, and thus provide a picture to identify effective public sector expenditure policies for poverty reduction and income distribution. Moreover, the inclusion of different components of the public sector capital investment in the SAM structure intends to strengthen the tool of the SAM-based short-term forecasting models so as to make them more effective in tracing the implications of the public expenditure adjustment policy. This then would help in better programming and monitoring of the development process.

Financial account analysis has been widely used in industrial economies as a basic information tool in general empirical research and for detailed policy analysis. However, relatively little work has been done for developing countries. Among the studies that incorporated financial accounts in their SAM in developing countries are Green and Murinde (2000), who developed a theoretical flow of funds model, and Green, Murinde, Suppakitjarak, and Moore (2000), who applied the model to conduct the analysis of financial policies for economy in developing countries. In a more recent study, Caldentey and Luzuriaga (2017) manifested the use of the flow-of-fund account matrices for the early 1990s recessions – the 1995 Mexican Tequila Crisis and the 1997–1999 Asian Crisis in six Latin American economies. Meanwhile, to trace the macro-financial interconnectedness of the economy for Spain, Aray, Pedauga, and Velâzquez (2017) incorporated the financial sector into the conventional SAM by comprising the breakdown of the asset and liability flows across the sectors.

In addition, Sen, Roy, Krishnan, and Mundlay (1996) analyzed a simple flow of funds model to explain the saving and investment behavior in India, while Honohan and Atiyas (1993) analyzed the flow of funds data for 17 developing countries. Agenor, Izquierdo, and Fofack (2003) explicitly incorporated the bank lending rate into the effective price of labor faced by firms that had to finance their labor requirements prior to the sale of their output. Fargeix and Sadoulet (1994), Lewis (1992, 1994) and Bourguignon, Branson, and Jaime de Melo (1992) analyzed linkages between bank credit and the supply side through working capital needs.

Khan's survey (2007) of the modeling of income distribution in a SAM modeling framework identified three generations of such models for developing economies. The first- and second-generation models included distributional issues but did not address poverty and financial market explicitly. The third-generation model did include the issue of poverty. However, with a few exceptions, the SAM models of the third generation still did not capture the structure of the financial markets. Financial SAM models for developing economics should be constructed in such a way that there will be a built-in capability for income distribution and poverty analysis. Khan said that financial SAM is the goal of the next phase of the modeling of distributional and poverty analysis.

This book differs from previous studies in two different ways. First, the book analyzes the impacts of public expenditure on income distribution by employing SAM. Second, the book incorporates the detailed disaggregation of public capital investment by sectors in the SAM.

3.3   Malaysian Macro SAM

Table 3.1 shows the circular flow of the economy in a single accounting framework. An aggregation of all the transaction details of the sectors has turned out a single macroeconomic transaction. The macro SAM is a compilation of four major categories, including production activities, institutions that cover household, company and public sectors, indirect taxes and the rest of world (ROW). The schematic SAM is viewed as a systematic data system. Thus, the distributional income among economic agents can be detected by looking at the flows around the schematic SAM, equipping initial information on production structure, capital distribution, value-added payment, institutional income distribution, tax structure and external flows.

In the SAM, the output for each account is spread along the row of the table while the corresponding column displays the input of this account. The production sectors created wide-ranging sectoral goods and services with the gross value of the output totaling RM2,757,388 million to various groups of intermediate and final users. The production sectors sold their output within or to other industries as intermediate input for RM1,221,227 million, to the households for RM556,670 million and the government as the final consumption (RM123,759 million) and investment (RM23,251 million) of domestic commodities and to the private sector as capital (RM206,096 million) and to the ROW as export (RM638,834 million). To produce the total amount of output, production sectors had to demand raw materials from domestic production sectors (RM1,221,227 million) and imports (RM395,544 million). Meanwhile, they had to pay indirect taxes to the government (RM20, 999) and factor payments to the households (RM412,240 million) and the company (RM707,378 million).

Besides, the accumulation of the income of the institutions is recorded along the row accounts while the respective columns show the allocations of institutional incomes. The households obtained factor incomes in the forms of wages and other labor incomes in exchange for the ownership of their services amounting to RM412,240 million; distributed profits and transfer from companies came to RM174,754 million, transfer from the government was RM18,872 million and transfer from the ROW was RM76,033 million. The total amount of income the households had was RM681,899 million. Their generated incomes were then allocated to the consumption of domestic commodities worth RM556,670 million and RM89,677 million on imported commodities, saving RM8,550 million as well as not paying income tax (RM26,321 million) and commodities taxes (RM681 million).

Companies are the entities that have capital stock and hence gain profits of RM707,378 million and non-factor income of RM42,270 million from abroad. From their incomes, they paid commodities taxes

Table 3.1 Malaysian Macro SAM

RM million		1 Production sectors	2 Households	3 Companies	4 Public current expenditure on domestic commodities	5 Public capital investment on domestic commodities	6 Indirect tax	7 Public current	8 Public capital	9 Private capital	10 Changes in inventory	11 ROW current	12 ROW capital	13 Total
Production sectors	1	1,221,227	556,670		123,759	23,251				206,096	(12,449)	638,834		2,757,388
Households	2	412,240		174,754	18,872							76,033		681,899
Companies	3	707,378										42,270		749,648
Public current expenditure on domestic commodities	4							142,631						142,631
Public capital investment on domestic commodities	5								23,251					23,251
Indirect tax	6	20,999	681	10,737								7,769		53,670
Public current	7		26,321	63,679			53,670		756	12,728		35,634		179,304
Public capital	8							35,155					21,477	56,632
Private capital	9		8,550	266,217									40,358	315,125
Changes in inventory	10			(12,449)										−12448.78
ROW current	11	395,544	89,677	188,625				1,518	32,625	96,301		88,592		892,882
ROW capital	12			58,085								3,750		61,835
Total	13	2,757,388	681,899	749,648	142,631	23,251	53,670	179,304	56,632	315,125	−12448.78	892,882	61,835	

(RM10,737 million), corporate taxes to the government (RM63,679 million), factorial and non-factorial income from abroad (RM188,625 million) and net investment abroad (RM58,085 million). Their residual saving was channeled into capital account (RM266,217 million).

The crucial role that the public sector played in the redistribution process was somehow well embedded in the conventional economic approach. In doing so, the public sector was distinguished with two major accounts, namely, current account and capital account. On the one hand, the public current account accumulated direct taxes from the households (RM26,321 million) and the companies (RM63,679 million), indirect taxes (RM53,670 million) and non-factor income from abroad (RM35,634 million). The accumulated revenues of RM179,304 million were then spent on buying the goods and services provided by the domestic production activities (RM142,631 million) and imported commodities (RM1,518 million). The remaining savings (or current account surplus) was transferred to the public capital account (RM35,155 million). Together with the external sources (RM21,477 million), the capital account distributed its investments on domestic production activities (RM206,096 million), capital taxes (RM12,728 million) and imported capital goods from the ROW (RM96,301 million).

The private sector earned its capital from household savings (RM8,550 million), company savings (RM266,217,550 million) and the source from abroad (RM40,358 million).

After all, the ROW account included transactions between domestic and foreign residents. On the ROW expense side, there were Malaysian households, companies and government consumption expenditure on imports which were final goods and capitals. The economy generated incomes from the ROW from exports, factor and non-factor income earned, and export and import levies. In focusing on the distribution of income, it was crucial to keep track of the separate flow between the institutions and the ROW.

3.4   Malaysian SAM (Disaggregated)

Table 3.5 presents the detailed framework of Malaysia's SAM 2015, 49 × 49 matrix accounts. The level of disaggregation of the individual account depended crucially on the question that SAM was expected to answer. In this case, the impact of public expenditure on income distribution brought the importance of the composition of the public expenditure, different categories of production activities, household inter-ethnic disparity and the urban–rural bias, which captured the different dimensions of income inequality. The disaggregation captured how changes in the public expenditure policy that affected various production structures were transmitted to the household sectors.

As the treatment of public expenditure was of particular interest, the framework incorporated a detailed breakdown of the public sector current expenditure and the public capital expenditure. An essential point in this context was not only that a larger aggregate public expenditure and investments that day might generate a higher aggregate output the next day, but also that the pattern and destination of expenditure and investment might be more important determinants of future equity and growth. The government's commitment to income distribution mattered most to the public spending patterns. Hence, the composition of public expenditure was specified and matched with the aggregation in the production sectors. It showed the extent to which public resource allocation decisions affected the distribution of income. The total public sector current expenditure was subdivided into six programs, classified by functions on the current expenditure in: agriculture and rural development (29), education (30), health (31), general administration (32), public defense and security (33), other public administration (34) and public transfer (35). In addition, public capital expenditure was subdivided into seven groups, covering public investment in agricultural and rural development (36), industry (37), trade (38), transportation and communication (39), education and health (40) public general administration (41) and other public investments (42).

The account of the various production sectors was very crucial in this SAM as the public sector affected income distribution through transmitting its expenditure to the households sector by purchaing from various production sectors. For government purchases, companies received higher profits than from non-government purchases, and consequently, stockholders and workers in those sectors, respectively, *ceteris paribus*, received higher dividends and higher wages. In this SAM, the production sector was aggregated to 18 × 18 production sectors. They were (1) agriculture; (2) mining and quarrying; (3) manufacturing; (4) electricity, gas and water; (5) building and constructions; (6) wholesale and retail trade; (7) hotel and restaurant; (8) transport; (9) communication; (10) financial, real estate and business; (11) business services; (12) education; (13) health; (14) recreation; (15) other private services; (16) public administration; (17) pubic order and defense and (18) other public administration.

Related to the income distribution analysis, the framework emphasized most notably the household group differentiation in the transmission of the public expenditure policy to the poor. The disaggregation of the household sector could capture how changes in various production structures, due to the public sector expenditure purchase, were transmitted to the household sector. There were nine household groups in the model, covering rural Malays (19), rural Chinese (20), rural Indians (21), rural others (22), urban Malays (23), urban Chinese (24), urban Indians (25), urban others (26) and

Table 3.2 Malaysian SAM

RM million		Agriculture	Mining & quarrying	Manufacturing	Electricity, gas & water	Buildings and construction	Wholesale and retail trade
		1	2	3	4	5	6
Agriculture	1	3,731.12	0	54,484.07	0	0	3,433.34
Mining & quarrying	2	26.9	10,016.94	56,399.29	334.6	3,703.84	5.39
Manufacturing	3	14,247.37	5,571.26	3,37,274.3	8,925.43	61,658.8	4,10,14.55
Electricity, gas & water	4	414.5	249.85	22,193.38	4,152.79	495.46	6,334.89
Building and constructions	5	148.26	1,094.06	785.59	5,724.89	6,713.3	7,704.74
Wholesale and retail trade	6	3,746.28	3,198.13	1,02,369.3	2,642.5	13,272.58	10,013.34
Hotel & restaurant	7	373.79	260.7	1,830.69	16.7	80.22	0
Transport	8	619.73	1,089.17	17,876.67	387.25	5,073.8	1,411
Communication	9	166.26	560.53	4,264.09	344.62	1,384.32	3,092.05
Financial, real estate & business	10	2,462.83	1,972.74	32,331.23	1,431.92	8,256.73	24,528.2
Business services	11	80.28	16.92	2,793.24	103.56	487.19	1,985.3
Education	12	0	0	0	0	0	0
Health	13	0	0	0	0	0	0
Recreation	14	0	0	0	0	0	0
Other private services	15	3.12	0.46	0	265.89	213.7	254.03
Public administration	16	0	0	0	0	0	0
Public order and defense	17	0	0	0	0	0	0
Other public administration	18	0	0	0	0	0	0
Rural Malays	19	10,845.41	936.8	1,0258.66	920.75	5,439.26	4,521.51
Rural Chinese	20	1,241.29	77.96	1,356.18	36.45	595.49	1,232.02
Rural Indians	21	289.66	50.29	508.38	32.6	82.25	180.21
Rural others	22	142.05	3.14	32.11	3.17	16.34	32.09
Urban Malays	23	3,059.14	6,730.11	38,247.3	3,464.35	15,231.52	17,947.64

24	Urban Chinese	1,943.05	752.78	28,339.27	71.38	13,940.55	25,576.33
25	Urban Indians	453.43	485.66	10,623.23	63.84	1,925.44	2,489.68
26	Urban others	222.35	30.35	670.94	6.21	382.57	666.12
27	Non-citizen	1,133.39	151.45	1,992.96	358.07	701.1	248.74
28	Companies	78,049.28	92,842.51	1,52,849.5	26,371.02	13,828.52	1,25,618.2
29	GovExpAgri&RurDev	0	0	0	0	0	0
30	GovExpEdu	0	0	0	0	0	0
31	GovExpHealth	0	0	0	0	0	0
32	GovExpGenAdmin	0	0	0	0	0	0
33	GovExpDef&Sec	0	0	0	0	0	0
34	GovExpOthers	0	0	0	0	0	0
35	GovExpTransfers	0	0	0	0	0	0
36	GovInvAgri&RurDev	0	0	0	0	0	0
37	GovInvIndustry	0	0	0	0	0	0
38	GovInvTrade	0	0	0	0	0	0
39	GovInvTransp.&Comm	0	0	0	0	0	0
40	GovInvEdu&Health	0	0	0	0	0	0
41	GovInvGenAdmin	0	0	0	0	0	0
42	GovInvOthers	0	0	0	0	0	0
43	Indirect taxes	498.08	620.38	9,863.76	453.13	1,632.88	2,057.84
44	Public current	0	0	0	0	0	0
45	Public capital	0	0	0	0	0	0
46	Private capital	0	0	0	0	0	0
47	Changes in inventory	0	0	0	0	0	0
48	ROW current	7,904.61	3,401.58	2,76,911.4	8,568.05	25,736.39	20,858.44
49	ROW capital	0	0	0	0	0	0
50	TOTAL	13,1802.2	13,0113.8	1,16,4256	64,679.17	18,0852.3	3,01,205.70

(Continued)

Table 3.2 (Continued)

RM million		Hotel & restaurant	Transport.	Comm.	Financial, real estate & bus.	Business Services	Education
		7	8	9	10	11	12
Agriculture	1	5,250.2	0	0	0	0	0
Mining & quarrying	2	0	0	0	0	0	0
Manufacturing	3	18,217.87	16,811.71	13,710.39	7,504.9	1,541.46	5,083.81
Electricity, gas & water	4	1,738.31	145.48	1,404.71	1,005.89	134.02	2,305.81
Building and constructions	5	231.35	86.51	3,658.32	5,008.83	603.3	624.85
Wholesale and retail trade	6	5,399.17	3,149.16	2,987.38	1,703.1	305.85	1,478.44
Hotel & restaurant	7	2,873.31	2,014.62	2,147.15	1,052.54	751.97	1,010.3
Transport	8	1,022.82	933.19	1,627.47	2,048.11	707.37	506.06
Communication	9	846.98	7,267.95	32,942.5	2,085.01	211.49	1,004.1
Financial, real estate & business	10	2,671.17	3,899.09	9,658.72	40,419.55	5,275.48	3,096.09
Business services	11	324.48	1,539.05	1,410.78	1,047.95	2,324.13	132.83
Education	12	0	0	0	0	0	899.42
Health	13	0	0	0	0	0	0
Recreation	14	70.96	0	0	0	0	71.61
Other private services	15	32.52	245.17	685.89	245.32	10.53	117.21
Public administration	16	0	0	0	0	0	4,154.33
Public order and defense	17	0	0	0	0	0	0
Other public administration	18	0	0	0	0	0	0
Rural Malays	19	1,868.58	1,152.44	650.95	1,206.61	219.66	9,892.56
Rural Chinese	20	317.46	132.83	112.05	188.16	19.62	235.8
Rural Indians	21	48.66	134.15	36.31	49.36	2.32	90.63
Rural others	22	12.02	6.85	1.1	2.21	0.12	7.57
Urban Malays	23	6,563.62	4,888.61	11,208.5	18,195.38	1,812.42	22,672.76

24 Urban Chinese	4,882.25	1,524.34	8,107.16	15,251.01	1,860.42	3,887.59
25 Urban Indians	748.32	1,539.5	2,626.9	4,000.68	220.36	1,494.11
26 Urban others	184.81	78.56	79.26	178.37	11.48	124.75
27 Non-citizen	160.48	51.15	183.54	134.4	26.08	155.46
28 Companies	18,955.15	11,990.95	56,266.73	10,1389.5	4,017.3	5,983.56
29 GovExpAgri&RurDev	0	0	0	0	0	0
30 GovExpEdu	0	0	0	0	0	0
31 GovExpHealth	0	0	0	0	0	0
32 GovExpGenAdmin	0	0	0	0	0	0
33 GovExpDefSec	0	0	0	0	0	0
34 GovExpOthers	0	0	0	0	0	0
35 GovExpTransfers	0	0	0	0	0	0
36 GovInvAgri&RurDev	0	0	0	0	0	0
37 GovInvIndustry	0	0	0	0	0	0
38 GovInvTrade	0	0	0	0	0	0
39 GovInvTransp.&Comm	0	0	0	0	0	0
40 GovInvEdu&Health	0	0	0	0	0	0
41 GovInvGenAdmin	0	0	0	0	0	0
42 GovInvOthers	0	0	0	0	0	0
43 Indirect taxes	906.83	699.04	1,838.08	1,644.74	250.11	94.51
44 Public current	0	0	0	0	0	0
45 Public capital	0	0	0	0	0	0
46 Private capital	0	0	0	0	0	0
47 Changes in inventory	0	0	0	0	0	0
48 ROW current	6,548.34	7,349.45	11,916.06	12,855.66	1,387.1	1,936.61
49 ROW capital	0	0	0	0	0	0
50 TOTAL	79,875.66	65,639.8	16,32.60	21,7217.2	21,692.59	67,060.77

(Continued)

Table 3.2 (Continued)

RM million		Health	Recreation	Other private services	Public admin.	Public order and defense	Other public admin.
		13	14	15	16	17	18
Agriculture	1	0	0	0	0	0	0
Mining & quarrying	2	0	0	0	0	0	0
Manufacturing	3	6,790.61	1,977.3	336.12	4,262.27	3,609.34	323.44
Electricity, gas & water	4	1,967.6	822.08	82.54	1,960.89	605.67	351.71
Building and constructions	5	274.36	192.82	0	1,902.3	517.95	33.22
Wholesale and retail trade	6	1,480.9	466.88	99.6	1,250.55	727.71	124.79
Hotel & restaurant	7	831.55	772.37	14.05	1,695.29	1,159.9	103.18
Transport	8	518.16	66.69	10.10	2,682.50	384.44	68.06
Communication	9	203.52	1,197.84	1,384.38	1,087.88	1,879.56	114.7
Financial, real estate & business	10	2,323.05	3,701.3	835.57	3,478.70	1,102.23	149.57
Business services	11	162.54	504.36	174.67	184.10	28.52	152.55
Education	12	42.35	0	0	0.058	1,161.23	0.11
Health	13	8,458.3	0	0	0	0	0
Recreation	14	761.49	128	0	109.25	28.07	63.03
Other private services	15	109.15	59.3	575.88	201.45	221.25	2.05
Public administration	16	288.03	0	0	0.391	4,308.73	0.78
Public order and defense	17	0	0	0	0	0	0
Other public administration	18	0	0	0	0	0	0
Rural Malays	19	2,346.01	312.94	287.86	11,331.87	3,541.58	1,163.48
Rural Chinese	20	16.16	3.01	79.43	301.14	108.41	48.14
Rural Indians	21	9.28	0	21.92	321.26	141.76	29.09
Rural others	22	0.64	0	0.95	20.52	36.69	6.02
Urban Malays	23	7,877.54	1,013.03	776.32	1,3279.69	5,056.11	1,721.14

24	Urban Chinese	3,036.42	792.74	794.3	2,814.04	897.95	377.13
25	Urban Indians	1,742.75	9.51	219.23	3,002.13	1,174.24	134.4
26	Urban others	119.48	234.65	9.53	191.78	303.92	7.02
27	Non-citizen	159.48	7.02	19.06	8.02	345.03	5.01
28	Companies	4,951.28	6,570.44	2,464.76	3,136.59	1,789.17	303.75
29	GovExpAgri&RurDev	0	0	0	0	0	0
30	GovExpEdu	0	0	0	0	0	0
31	GovExpHealth	0	0	0	0	0	0
32	GovExpGenAdmin	0	0	0	0	0	0
33	GovExpDef&Sec	0	0	0	0	0	0
34	GovExpOthers	0	0	0	0	0	0
35	GovExpTransfers	0	0	0	0	0	0
36	GovInvAgri&RurDev	0	0	0	0	0	0
37	GovInvIndustry	0	0	0	0	0	0
38	GovInvTrade	0	0	0	0	0	0
39	GovInvTransp&Comm	0	0	0	0	0	0
40	GovInvEdu&Health	0	0	0	0	0	0
41	GovInvGenAdmin	0	0	0	0	0	0
42	GovInvOthers	0	0	0	0	0	0
43	Indirect taxes	133.12	221.88	84.16	0	0	0.04
44	Public current	0	0	0	0	0	0
45	Public capital	0	0	0	0	0	0
46	Private capital	0	0	0	0	0	0
47	Changes in inventory	0	0	0	0	0	0
48	ROW current	2,463.47	2,157.77	108.24	2,613.00	2,701.87	126.06
49	ROW capital	0	0	0	0	0	0
50	TOTAL	47,067.24	21,211.93	8,378.67	55,835.67	31,831.33	5,408.47

(Continued)

Table 3.2 (Continued)

RM million		Rural Malay	Rural Chinese	Rural Indian	Rural others	Urban Malay	Urban Chinese
		19	20	21	22	23	24
Agriculture	1	6,865.00	825.85	280.17	456.77	20,108.98	13,371.89
Mining & quarrying	2	0	0	0	0	0	0
Manufacturing	3	28,391.53	2,448.82	784.00	1,282.21	71,171.15	45,842.21
Electricity, gas & water	4	3,291.83	319.77	96.45	117.30	7,899.62	4,414.74
Building and constructions	5	0	0	0	0	0	0
Wholesale and retail trade	6	8,020.01	608.97	154.9	225.84	21,045.53	12,374.97
Hotel & restaurant	7	11,337.86	988.12	259.77	273	27,388.11	16,263.16
Transport	8	1,298.36	174.47	16.92	67.95	1,697	1,183.74
Communication	9	12,588.00	1,165.62	304.33	410.08	29,295.64	17,524.26
Financial, real estate & business	10	10,009.35	1,035.03	174.96	351.2	21,933.11	15,818.22
Business services	11	1,418.98	111.38	26.36	47.61	2,987.61	2,639.86
Education	12	5,611.34	201.78	153.96	65.77	11,343.78	7,624.81
Health	13	4,176.75	358.76	107.12	78.24	8,625.46	6,071.20
Recreation	14	3,701.6	234.43	88.33	72.7	6,887.49	5,784.19
Other private services	15	677.53	47.64	21.74	4.19	2,833.42	904.53
Public administration	16	0	0	0	0	0	0
Public order and defense	17	0	0	0	0	0	0
Other public administration	18	0	0	0	0	0	0
Rural Malays	19	0	0	0	0	0	0
Rural Chinese	20	0	0	0	0	0	0
Rural Indians	21	0	0	0	0	0	0
Rural others	22	0	0	0	0	0	0
Urban Malays	23	0	0	0	0	0	0

Urban Chinese	24	0	0	0	0	0	0
Urban Indians	25	0	0	0	0	0	0
Urban others	26	0	0	0	0	0	0
Non-citizen	27	0	0	0	0	0	0
Companies	28	0	0	0	0	0	0
GovExpAgri&RurDev	29	0	0	0	0	0	0
GovExpEdu	30	0	0	0	0	0	0
GovExpHealth	31	0	0	0	0	0	0
GovExpGenAdmin	32	0	0	0	0	0	0
GovExpDef&Sec	33	0	0	0	0	0	0
GovExpOthers	34	0	0	0	0	0	0
GovExpTransfers	35	0	0	0	0	0	0
GovInvAgri&RurDev	36	0	0	0	0	0	0
GovInvIndustry	37	0	0	0	0	0	0
Gov.InvTrade	38	0	0	0	0	0	0
GovInvTransp.&Comm	39	0	0	0	0	0	0
GovInv.Edu&Health	40	0	0	0	0	0	0
GovInvGenAdmin	41	0	0	0	0	0	0
GovInvOthers	42	0	0	0	0	0	0
Indirect taxes	43	118.670	10.310	3.040	4.200	285.990	182.910
Public current	44	4,280	573	65	31	13,944.0	5,570.0
Public capital	45	0	0	0	0	0	0
Private capital	46	1,366.670	133.700	32.710	42.980	3,924.670	2,227.490
Changes in inventory	47	0	0	0	0	0	0
ROW current	48	28,678.00	4,651.68	465.14	907.82	37,341.04	13,916.12
ROW capital	49	0	0	0	0	0	0
TOTAL	50	1,31,831.5	13,889.33	3,034.9	4,438.86	2,88,712.6	1,71,714.3

(Continued)

Table 3.2 (Continued)

RM million		Urban Indian	Urban others	Non-citizen	Company	GovExpAgri&RurDev	GovExpEdu
		25	26	27	28	29	30
Agriculture	1	4,143.84	1,017.07	660.18	0	2,039.64	0
Mining & quarrying	2	0	0	0	0	0	0
Manufacturing	3	1,6019.23	3,039.47	1,944.39	0	0	0
Electricity, gas & water	4	1,606.13	335.49	220.22	0	0	0
Building and constructions	5	0	0	0	0	0	0
Wholesale and retail trade	6	3,841.48	770.81	726.98	0	0	0
Hotel & restaurant	7	4,729.71	947.41	700.19	0	0	0
Transport	8	372.26	51.73	184.61	0	0	0
Communication	9	4,603.73	1,111.6	1,099.85	0	0	0
Financial, real estate & business	10	3,488.41	831.23	876.52	0	0	0
Business services	11	601.09	201.50	205.75	0	0	0
Education	12	1,523.16	435.08	413.02	0	0	34,189.87
Health	13	1,979.43	414.13	358.45	0	0	0
Recreation	14	1,052.24	456.32	195.26	0	0	0
Other private services	15	527.59	73.57	45.54	0	0	0
Public administration	16	0	0	0	0	0	0
Public order and defense	17	0	0	0	0	0	0
Other public administration	18	0	0	0	0	0	0
Rural Malays	19	0	0	0	42,427.62	0	0
Rural Chinese	20	0	0	0	6,076.79	0	0
Rural Indians	21	0	0	0	366.92	0	0
Rural others	22	0	0	0	2,882.19	0	0
Urban Malays	23	0	0	0	71,870.13	0	0

Urban Chinese	24	0	0	0	41,604.64	0
Urban Indians	25	0	0	0	6,062.96	0
Urban others	26	0	0	0	2,079.1	0
Non-citizen	27	0	0	0	1,383.74	0
Companies	28	0	0	0	0	0
GovExpAgri&RurDev	29	0	0	0	0	0
GovExpEdu	30	0	0	0	0	0
GovExpHealth	31	0	0	0	0	0
GovExpGenAdmin	32	0	0	0	0	0
GovExpDef&Sec	33	0	0	0	0	0
GovExpOthers	34	0	0	0	0	0
GovExpTransfers	35	0	0	0	0	0
GovInvAgri&RurDev	36	0	0	0	0	0
GovInvIndustry	37	0	0	0	0	0
GovInvTrade	38	0	0	0	0	0
GovInv.Transp.&Comm	39	0	0	0	0	0
GovInv.Edu&Health	40	0	0	0	0	0
GovInvGenAdmin	41	0	0	0	0	0
GovInvOthers	42	0	0	0	0	0
Indirect taxes	43	54.710	11.890	9.290	10,737.00	0
Public current	44	958	454	446	63,679.00	0
Public capital	45	0	0	0	0	0
Private capital	46	570.830	152.920	98.040	2,66,217.00	0
Changes in inventory	47	0	0	0	−12,448.87	0
ROW current	48	1,790.51	830.37	1,096.50	1,88,625.00	0
ROW capital	49	0	0	0	58,085.00	0
TOTAL	50	47,862.35	11,134.59	9,280.79	7,49,648.2	2,039.64	34,189.87

(Continued)

Table 3.2 (Continued)

RM million		GovExp Health	GovExpGen Admin	GovExpDef & Sec	GovExp Others	GovExp Transfers	GovInvAgri & RuralDev	GovInv Industry
		31	32	33	34	35	36	37
Agriculture	1	0	0	0	0	0	1,442.05	0
Mining & quarrying	2	0	0	0	0	0	0	0
Manufacturing	3	0	0	0	0	0	0	838
Electricity, gas & water	4	0	0	0	0	0	0	0
Building and constructions	5	0	0	0	30	0	0	0
Wholesale and retail trade	6	0	0	0	0	0	0	0
Hotel & restaurant	7	0	0	0	0	0	0	0
Transport	8	0	0	0	0	0	0	0
Communication	9	0	0	0	0	0	0	0
Financial, real estate & business	10	0	0	0	0	0	0	0
Business services	11	0	0	0	0	0	0	0
Education	12	0	0	0	0	0	0	0
Health	13	15,346.4	0	0	0	0	0	0
Recreation	14	0	0	0	0	0	0	0
Other private services	15	0	0	0	0	0	0	0
Public administration	16	0	40,694.8	0	0	0	0	0
Public order and defense	17	0	0	26,746	0	0	0	0
Other public administration	18	0	0	0	4,712.41	0	0	0
Rural Malays	19	0	0	0	0	9,426.97	0	0
Rural Chinese	20	0	0	0	0	541.98	0	0
Rural Indians	21	0	0	0	0	32.99	0	0
Rural others	22	0	0	0	0	258.02	0	0
Urban Malays	23	0	0	0	0	6,250.04	0	0

24	Urban Chinese	0	0	0	0	1,665.99	0	0
25	Urban Indians	0	0	0	0	510	0	0
26	Urban others	0	0	0	0	186.01	0	0
27	Non-citizen	0	0	0	0	0	0	0
28	Companies	0	0	0	0	0	0	0
29	GovExpAgri&RurDev	0	0	0	0	0	0	0
30	GovExpEdu	0	0	0	0	0	0	0
31	GovExpHealth	0	0	0	0	0	0	0
32	GovExpGenAdmin	0	0	0	0	0	0	0
33	GovExpDef&Sec	0	0	0	0	0	0	0
34	GovExpOthers	0	0	0	0	0	0	0
35	GovExpTransfers	0	0	0	0	0	0	0
36	GovInvAgri&RurDev	0	0	0	0	0	0	0
37	GovInvIndustry	0	0	0	0	0	0	0
38	GovInvTrade	0	0	0	0	0	0	0
39	GovInvTransp.&Comm	0	0	0	0	0	0	0
40	GovInv.Edu&Health	0	0	0	0	0	0	0
41	GovInvGenAdmin	0	0	0	0	0	0	0
42	GovInvOthers	0	0	0	0	0	0	0
43	Indirect taxes	0	0	0	0	0	0	0
44	Public current	0	0	0	0	0	0	0
45	Public capital	0	0	0	0	0	0	0
46	Private capital	0	0	0	0	0	0	0
47	Changes in inventory	0	0	0	0	0	0	0
48	ROW current	0	0	0	0	0	0	0
49	ROW capital	0	0	0	0	0	0	0
50	TOTAL	15,346.4	40,694.8	26,746.0	4,742.41	18,872.00	1,442.05	838.00

(Continued)

Table 3.2 (Continued)

RM million		GovInv Trade	GovInv Transp & Comm	GovInv Edu & Health	GovInv Gen Admin	GovInv Others	Indirect Tax	Public Current
		38	39	40	41	42	43	44
Agriculture	1	0	0	0	0	0	0	0
Mining & quarrying	2	0	0	0	0	3,447.99	0	0
Manufacturing	3	0	0	0	0	0	0	0
Electricity, gas & water	4	0	0	0	0	0	0	0
Building and constructions	5	1,387.19	0	0	0	0	0	0
Wholesale and retail trade	6	0	0	0	0	91	0	0
Hotel & restaurant	7	0	0	0	0	0	0	0
Transport	8	0	1,628.01	0	0	0	0	0
Communication	9	0	0	0	0	0	0	0
Financial, real estate & business	10	0	0	0	0	0	0	0
Business services	11	0	0	0	0	0	0	0
Education	12	0	0	3,395.09	0	0	0	0
Health	13	0	0	1,093.03	0	0	0	0
Recreation	14	0	0	0	0	0	0	0
Other private services	15	0	0	0	0	0	0	0
Public Administration	16	0	0	0	4,147.21	0	0	0
Public order and defense	17	0	0	0	5,085.37	0	0	0
Other public administration	18	0	0	0	0	696.06	0	0
Rural Malays	19	0	0	0	0	0	0	0
Rural Chinese	20	0	0	0	0	0	0	0
Rural Indians	21	0	0	0	0	0	0	0
Rural others	22	0	0	0	0	0	0	0
Urban Malays	23	0	0	0	0	0	0	0

No.	Account							
24	Urban Chinese	0	0	0	0	0	0	0
25	Urban Indians	0	0	0	0	0	0	0
26	Urban others	0	0	0	0	0	0	0
27	Non-citizen	0	0	0	0	0	0	0
28	Companies	0	0	0	0	0	0	0
29	GovExpAgri&RurDev	0	0	0	0	0	0	2,039.64
30	GovExpEdu	0	0	0	0	0	0	34,189.87
31	GovExpHealth	0	0	0	0	0	0	15,346.37
32	GovExpGenAdmin	0	0	0	0	0	0	40,694.75
33	GovExpDef&Sec	0	0	0	0	0	0	26,745.96
34	GovExpOthers	0	0	0	0	0	0	4,742.41
35	GovExpTransfers	0	0	0	0	0	0	18,872.00
36	GovInvAgric&RurDev	0	0	0	0	0	0	0
37	GovInvIndustry	0	0	0	0	0	0	0
38	GovInvTrade	0	0	0	0	0	0	0
39	GovInvTransp&Comm	0	0	0	0	0	0	0
40	GovInvEdu&Health	0	0	0	0	0	0	0
41	GovInvGenAdmin	0	0	0	0	0	0	0
42	GovInvOthers	0	0	0	0	0	0	0
43	Indirect taxes	0	0	0	0	0	53,669.6	0
44	Public Current	0	0	0	0	0	0	0
45	Public capital	0	0	0	0	0	0	35,155.00
46	Private capital	0	0	0	0	0	0	0
47	Changes in inventory	0	0	0	0	0	0	0
48	ROW current	0	0	0	0	0	0	1,518.00
49	ROW capital	0	0	0	0	0	0	0
50	TOTAL	1,387.19	1,628.01	4,488.12	9,232.58	4,235.05	53,669.6	179,304.00

(Continued)

Table 3.2 (Continued)

RM million		Public capital	Private capital	Changes in inventory	ROW current	ROW capital	TOTAL
		45	46	47	48	49	50
Agriculture	1	0	6,180.2	−1,829	9,340.81	0	1,31,802.18
Mining & quarrying	2	0	5,548.98	−1,058.98	51,688.82	0	1,30,113.77
Manufacturing	3	0	26,124.84	−16,328.59	4,33,837.4	0	1,164,255.64
Electricity, gas & water	4	0	0	8	4.04	0	64,679.17
Building and constructions	5	0	134,588.9	6,759.7	4,077.97	0	180,852.25
Wholesale and retail trade	6	0	12,857.89	0	84,775.43	0	3,01,205.69
Hotel & restaurant	7	0	0	0	0	0	79,875.66
Transport	8	0	1,139.01	0	20,793.15	0	65,639.80
Communication	9	0	15,185.03	0	19,934.03	0	1,63,259.95
Financial, real estate & business	10	0	2,733	0	12,372.03	0	217,217.23
Business services	11	0	0	0	0	0	21,692.59
Education	12	0	0	0	0	0	67,060.83
Health	13	0	0	0	0	0	47,067.24
Recreation	14	0	0	0	1,506.96	0	21,211.93
Other private services	15	0	0	0	0	0	8,378.67
Public administration	16	0	1,738.06	0	503.33	0	55,835.61
Public order and defense	17	0	0	0	0	0	31,831.33
Other public administration	18	0	0	0	0	0	5,408.47
Rural Malays	19	0	0	0	13,079.96	0	131,831.48
Rural Chinese	20	0	0	0	1,168.96	0	13,889.33
Rural Indians	21	0	0	0	606.86	0	3,034.90
Rural others	22	0	0	0	975.06	0	4,438.86
Urban Malays	23	0	0	0	30,847.25	0	288,712.60

24	Urban Chinese	0	0	0	13,594.96	0	171,714.30
25	Urban Indians	0	0	0	8,335.98	0	47,862.35
26	Urban others	0	0	0	5,367.33	0	11,134.59
27	Non-citizen	0	0	0	2,056.61	0	9,280.79
28	Companies	0	0	0	42,270.00	0	749,648.22
29	GovExpAgri&RurDev	0	0	0	0	0	2,039.64
30	GovExpEdu	0	0	0	0	0	34,189.87
31	GovExpHealth	0	0	0	0	0	15,346.37
32	GovExpGenAdmin	0	0	0	0	0	40,694.75
33	GovExpDef&Sec	0	0	0	0	0	26,745.96
34	GovExpOthers	0	0	0	0	0	4,742.41
35	GovExpTransfers	0	0	0	0	0	18,872.00
36	GovInvAgri&RurDev	1,442.05	0	0	0	0	1,442.05
37	GovInvIndustry	838.00	0	0	0	0	838.00
38	GovInvTrade	1,387.19	0	0	0	0	1,387.19
39	GovInvTransp&Comm	1,628.01	0	0	0	0	1,628.01
40	GovInvEdu&Health	4,488.12	0	0	0	0	4,488.12
41	GovInvGenAdmin	9,232.58	0	0	0	0	9,232.58
42	GovInvOthers	4,235.05	0	0	0	0	4,235.05
43	Indirect taxes	756.00	12,728.00	0	7,769.00	0	53,669.59
44	Public current	0	0	0	35,634.41	0	179,304.00
45	Public capital	0	0	0	0	21,477.00	56,632.00
46	Private capital	0	0	0	0	40,358.00	315,125.01
47	Changes in inventory	0	0	0	0	0	−12,448.87
48	ROW current	32,625.00	9,6301.07	0	88,592.13	0	892,882.51
49	ROW capital	0	0	0	3,750.00	0	61,835.00
50	TOTAL	56,632.00	31,5125	−12,448.87	89,2882.5	61,835.00	

non-citizens (27). This disaggregation of the household was based on socio-economic groups rather than on income levels. Being a multi-racial country, it was very crucial to distinguish four major ethnic groups for the household, namely, the Malays, the Chinese, the Indians and others.[1] This disaggregation was very important as income equality among the ethnic groups had been an important government development strategy since independence. Besides focusing on the income distribution among the ethnic groups, since the majority of the poor lived in rural areas, the distinction of households between the rural and urban areas was also very important. The urban–rural area disaggregation was useful since the distinction captured many aspects of duality.

The most notable feature of the Malaysia SAM was the incorporation of the detailed disaggregation of the public capital investments, which gave a view on the linkages between the public sector financial account and the real accounts. It showed how the use of public funds in the different segments in the economy could generate different levels of income for different household groups. For instance, the public capital investment in agriculture and rural development caused the agricultural sector to require labor, and in turn this labor required wages based on their factor ownership, thus bringing generation of income or output in that sector.

3.5   SAM Modeling

This section provides a model for inferring the functional distribution of income of the Malaysian SAM due to the public expenditure expansion programs. The model proposed is a SAM-based general equilibrium model, called the fixed-price multiplier model. The base methodology of the multiplier will be used in keeping with the work by Emini and Fofack (2004), Keuning and Thorbecke (1989), Pyatt and Round (1985, 1977), Defourny and Thorbecke (1984) and Kuburski (1973), which represent the basis of what has so far been done in this area.

$$Y_n = A_n * Y_n + Gg + Ff \tag{1}$$

A functional relationship between output and final demand may obtain:

$$Y_n = (I - A_n)^{-1}(Gg + Ff) \tag{2}$$

where
   Y_n is the total receipts of the endogenous accounts,
   $(I - A_n)^{-1}$ is the accounting multipliers,
   F is the $q \times s$ matrix of other final demand coefficients including consumption, investment and exports,

f– is the $s \times 1$ vector of the ringgit value of other final demand by source in the base year,

G– is the $n \times p$ matrix of the public sector expenditure coefficients, whose (i,j)th element is the ringgit of purchases from sector i per ringgit spent by jth class expenditure,

g – is the $p \times 1$ vector of the values of expenditure by class in the base year and

I– is the $n \times n$ identity matrix.

From equation (1), endogenous incomes Y_n can be derived by multiplying injection (g) by the multiplier matrix $(I - A_n)^{-1}$. This inverse matrix $(I - A_n)^{-1}$ indicates the total need for output in different industries so that one unit of public expenditure can be produced in the industry examined. Hence, they are the repercussions caused by the production of public expenditure on the output of different industries that are revealed by the inverse matrix.

The demand for 'primary input'[2] in the reference year is defined by the following equations:

$$D = BY_n + Hg + Ef \tag{3}$$

Where

D– is the $t \times 1$ vector of the total values of 'primary input' (indirect taxes, incomes, and surplus),

B– is the $t \times n$ matrix of primary input coefficients and

H *and* E – are direct primary input coefficients of appropriate order associated with the public sector and other final demands.

Substituting Y_n for (3) yields the following relationship between 'primary input' demand and final demand.

$$D = B(1 - A_n)^{-1}(Gg + Ff) + Hg + Ef \tag{4}$$

Assuming a change only in public expenditures by class, the result is

$$\Delta D = B(I - A_n)^{-1}G\Delta g + H\Delta g \tag{5}$$

The public sector expenditure by different classes will generate different mixes of indirect taxes, labor income and surplus.

In the multiplier analysis, for any public expenditure injection anywhere in the SAM, influence is transmitted through the interdependent SAM system. The total, direct and indirect effects of the increase in public expenditure on the endogenous accounts are estimated through the multiplier process. Due to the increase in public expenditure, the government will demand more input from different sectors, employment will increase in both the private and public sectors and accordingly, there will be an increase in the demand for consumption goods. These effects work through the economy via inter-sectoral linkages.

3.6   Policy Experiments

By varying the pattern of the exogenous public sector expenditure, the impact on the whole socioeconomic system and, in particular on income distribution, can be estimated. This amounts to postulating different alternative expenditure matrices and measuring their effects on endogenous incomes. In other words, varying the matrix of public expenditure and pre-multiplying the injections by M_a yields the corresponding total incomes of the 43 endogenous variables appearing in the Malaysian SAM. Both direct and indirect effects are generated by the public expenditure (injections) circulating throughout the economy and these total effects are in principle captured by the multiplier matrix. The key assumption, which is made throughout the analysis, is that the multiplier matrix accurately captures and reflects the structural and behavioral features of the Malaysian economy. The experiments below are to show the different patterns of exogenous public sector expenditure.

Experiment 0: Base year 2015 experiments using actual exogenous demand matrixes from the 2015 SAM transaction matrix. The base year scenario is used as the reference scenario. The matrix of the exogenous injections is referred to as 'x.' For the base year 2015, this matrix appears in Table 4.4 (see rows 1–43 and columns 44–49). The 'x' is thus a 43×6 matrix. If the subscript o refers to the base year (2015) values, x_0 is the actual 2015 exogenous injection matrix. The following relationship can be obtained: $Y_0 = M_a x_0$, where M_a (43×43) is the fixed price multiplier matrix for 2015. In turn Y_0 would be the 43×6 matrix of the endogenous receipts generated by the injection matrix x_0. It yields the endogenous receipts for each of the 43 endogenous categories of the SAM generated directly or indirectly by each of the six exogenous injections. Thus, one can break down what part of the total income of a given household group (say rural Malays) could be ascribed in the multiplier process to the government's current and capital expenditure and four other exogenous injections. By summing the rows of, one obtains the resulting total income of each of the 43 endogenous categories. In addition to the base year scenario experiment, two alternative experiments were simulated as follows:

Experiment 1: Reflects the actual (realized) average public expenditure prevailing during the Eleventh Malaysia Plan. Thus, in particular, the level and composition of the public sector current and capital expenditure among the 14 programs corresponded to the actual public expenditure allocation and realization during the Eleventh Malaysia Plan. If subscript 1 refers to the public sector's current and capital expenditure during the Eleventh Malaysia Plan's values and six other exogenous injections, x_1 is the new exogenous injection matrix. The following relationship can be obtained: $Y_1 = M_a x_1$, where M_a (43×43) is the fixed price multiplier matrix for 2015. In turn, Y_1 would be a 43×6 matrix of the endogenous receipts generated by the injection matrix x_1.

Experiment 2: Equiproportional public expenditure expansion in 2015. Each individual category of the public current expenditure in 2015 would increase by the same proportion as the total public current expenditure growth in the Eleventh Malaysia Plan for the base year 2015. It entailed an equal proportional growth in each individual program of the current expenditure of 33.6 percent. Meanwhile, each individual category of capital investments in 2015 would increase by the same proportion as the total public capital investment growth in the Eleventh Malaysia Plan for the base year 2015. It entailed an equal proportional growth in each individual program of the capital investment of 55.8 percent. If subscript 2 refers to the equiproportional public current and capital expenditure expansion in 2015 values, x_2 is the new exogenous injection matrix. The following relationship can be obtained: $Y_2 = M_a x_2$, where M_a is the fixed-price multiplier matrix for 2015. In turn, Y_5 would be a 43×6 matrix of the endogenous receipts generated by the injection matrix x_2.

3.7 Conclusion

This chapter delineated the features and characteristics of the constructed SAM structure on the subject of income distribution. The incorporation of different compositions of public expenditure in the SAM provided a base to identify effective public sector expenditure policies for poverty reduction and income distribution. To date, there is still comparatively little attention paid to public expenditure, just linked to the distribution of income in Malaysia, especially incorporating financial information into the model.

This model is a compilation of four main categories, which are production activities, institutions that cover households, the company and the public sector, indirect taxes and the ROW. The notable characteristic of the constructed SAM can be seen in the public expenditure on households and production activities in order to reach the objective of the study. First and foremost, the inclusion of the detailed composition of the public sector capital investment would allow one to examine more precisely how the use of public funds to different segments in the economy enhances the income inequality of the country, besides working on the disaggregation of public current expenditure. On top of that, the household is assumed as an institutional unit that represents all the people in the society. They are behaviorally distinct units that make economic decisions about the supply of labor and consumption expenditure. Meanwhile, poverty or the welfare of the society is expressed in terms of per-capita household income and consumption in the study. To examine the distribution of income among the ethnic groups across the region, nine socioeconomic household segments are distinguished according to different ethnic groups and rural versus urban, together with one non-citizen. There are 18 production sectors that are the aggregation of 124 production activities (provided by the latest Malaysian input–output table for 2015). Other accounts cover companies, the public sector, the private sector and the ROW.

This constructed SAM provides a crucial data source for the policy experiments. It allows quantifying the impact of the public expenditure expansion programs (by referring to the Eleventh Malaysia Plan) on the whole socioeconomic structure and, in particular income distribution. By keeping the work consistent with Emini and Fofack (2004), Keuning and Thorbecke (1989), Pyatt and Round (1985, 1977), Defourny and Thorbecke (1984) and Kubursi (1973), the policy experiments were solved using the multiplier analysis.

Notes

1 Other groups were minority ethnic groups who were mostly located in east Malaysia such as the Iban, Kadazan, Bajau and Murut.
2 Primary input refers to indirect taxes, incomes and surplus.

References

Agenor, P. R., Izquierdo, A., & Fofack, H. (2003). *IMMPA: A quantitative macroeconomic framework for the analysis of poverty reduction strategies*. Washington, DC: The World Bank.

Ahluwia, M. S. & Lysy, J. (1979). *A general equilibrium model of Malaysia*. Mimeo: Developing Research Center, World Bank.

Aray, H., Pedauga, L., & Velâzquez, A. (2017). Financial social accounting matrix: A useful tool for understanding the macro-financial linkages of an economy. *Economic Systems Resèarch, 29*(4), 486–508.

Bourguignon, F., Branson, W. H., & de Melo, J. (1992, January). Adjustment and income distribution. *Journal of Development Economics, 38*, 17–39.

Caldentey, E. P., & Luzuriaga, M. C. (2017). *Monitoring the evolution of Latin American economies using a flow-of-funds framework* (ECLAC-Financing for Developing Series No. 265). Mexico, DF: Economic Commission for Latin America and the Caribbean.

Defourny, J., & Thorbecke, E. (1984). Structural path analysis and multiplier decomposition within a Social Accounting Matrix framework. *The Economics Journal, 94*, 111–136.

Emini, C. A., & Fofack, H. (2004, February). *A financial Social Accounting Matrix for the integrated macroeconomic model for poverty analysis. Application to Cameroon with a fixed-price multiplier analysis* (Policy Research Working Paper No. 3210). Washington, DC: World Bank.

Fargeix, A., & Sadoulet, E. (1994). A financial computable general equilibrium model for the analysis of stabilization programs. In J. Mercenier & T. N. Srinivasan (Eds.), *Applied general equilibrium and economic development: Present achievements and future trends.* Michigan, US: University of Michigan Press.

Green, C. J., & Murinde, V. (2000). *Flow of funds: Implications for research on financial sector development and the real economy* (Economic Research Paper, No. 00/6). Loughborough, UK: Loughborough University.

Green, C. J., Murinde, V., Suppakitjarak, J., & Moore, T. (2000). *Compiling and understanding the flow of funds in developing countries* (Finance and Development Research Programme Working Paper Series No. 21). Manchester, UK: Institute for Development Policy and Management.

Honohan, P., & Atiyas, I. (1993). Intersectoral financial flows in developing countries. *The Economic Journal, 103*(418), 666–679.

Keuning, S., & Thorbecke, E. (1989). *The impact of budget retrenchment on income distribution in Indonesia: A Social Accounting Matrix application* (Working Paper No. 3). Paris, France: OECD Development Centre.

Khan, A. H. (2007). *Social Accounting Matrices (SAMs) and CGE modeling: Using macroeconomic computable general equilibrium models for assessing poverty impact of structural adjustment policies.* CIRJE Discussion Papers. Retrieved January, 2, 2007, from www.e.u-tokyo.ac.jp/cirje/research/03research02dp.html

Khor, H. E. (1982). *Income distribution and unemployment in Malaysia: A dual economy (CGE) model* [Doctoral dissertation, Princeton University]. Princeton, New Jersey: Princeton University.

Kubursi, A. A. (1973). Evaluating the economic impact of government expenditure by department an application of input-output analysis. *Socio-Economic Planning Sciences, 8*(2), 101–108. Pergamon Press.

Lewis, J. D. (1992). Financial repression and liberalization in a general equilibrium model with financial markets. *Journal of Policy Modeling, 14*, 135–166.

Lewis, J. D. (1994). Macroeconomic stabilization and adjustment policies in general equilibrium model with financial market: Turkey. In J. Mercenier & T. N. Srinivasan (Eds.), *Applied general equilibrium and economic development.* Michigan, US: University of Michigan Press.

Pyatt, G. (1991). SAMs, the SNA and national accounting capabilities. *Review of Income and Wealth, 17*, 177–198.

Pyatt, G., & Round, J. I. (1977). Social accounting for development planning. *Review of Income and Wealth, 23*, 339–364.

Pyatt, G., & Round, J. I. (1979). Accounting and fixed price multipliers in a Social Accounting Matrix framework. *The Economic Journal, 89*(356).

Pyatt, G., & Round, J. I. (Eds.). (1985). *Social accounting matrices: A basis for planning.* Washington, DC: The World Bank.

Pyatt, G., Round, J. I., & Denes, J. (1984). *Improving the macroeconomic database: a SAM for Malaysia, 1970.* Staff Working Paper, 646. Washington, DC: The World Bank.

Ramesh, C., Gnasegarah, S., Pyatt, G., & Round, J. I. (1980). Social accounts and distribution of income. The Malaysian economy in 1970. *Review of Income and Wealth, 26*(1).

Roland-Host, D., & Sancho, F. (1995). Modelling prices in SAM structure. *The Review of Economics and Statistics*, 361–371.

Saari, M. Y., Dietzenbacher, E., & Los, B. (2014). Income distribution across ethnic groups in Malaysia: Results from a new social accounting matrix. *Asian Economic Journal, 28*(3), 259–278.

Sen, K., Roy, T., Krishnan, R., & Mundlay, A. (1996). A flow of funds model for India and its implications. *Journal of Policy Modelling, 18*(5), 469–494.

Zakariah, A. R. (2005). *Social Accounting Matrix: Applications in policy formulation.* Paper presented at the National Statistic Conference 2005. Kuala Lumpur: Department of Statistics Malaysia.

4 Analysis on the Impact of Public Expenditure on Income Distribution

4.1 Introduction

SAM models provide a useful framework to analyze how the workings of the market mechanism determine the incomes of households. Changes in production brought about by the government purchase policy in particular sectors alter the distribution of income among the household groups.

Generally, the results show that there is a significant income inequality among ethnic groups and between the rural and urban areas, and public expenditure expansion has improved income inequality in Malaysia. The improvement in income inequality, however, varies in different periods because it very much depends on the pattern or composition of the public expenditure where the composition of public expenditure is closely linked to the public sector policies or commitment to income distribution.

Expenditure expansion in public transfer appears to have the most significant impact in improving income inequality and it is followed by the expansion in public current expenditure on education, public current expenditure on health, public investment in education and health, public current expenditure on general administration and public investment in general administration. On the contrary, expansion in public investment in the wholesale and retail trade, industry, and transportation and communication has low impacts on improving income inequality. Although public investment in agriculture and rural development has a low impact on the incomes of all ethnic groups, it still benefits the Malay households more compared to other ethnic groups and it has the potential to improve income equality.

The remaining chapter is organized as follows: Section 4.2 focuses on the initial functional and institutional distribution of income that comes from the statistical basis of the SAM system. The discussion is then separated into three parts, which are distribution of resources in the country's economy (Section 4.2.1), public sector allocation of resources (Section 4.2.2) and household income distribution (Section 4.2.3). The empirical assessment of

DOI: 10.4324/9781003302506-4

the increasing public expenditure for the institutional income distribution is carried out in Section 4.3. Following this are the concluding remarks in Section 4.4.

4.2   Initial Functional and Institutional Distribution of Income

4.2.1   *Distribution of Resources in Malaysian Economy*

Table SAM (Table 3.2) shows the value terms of the various economic flows within the economy during 2015, the base year. This is the transaction table, which shows the statistical basis of the SAM system. The output for each account is distributed along the rows of the table while the corresponding columns record the input of this account.

Table 4.1 provides the estimation of the composition of the sectoral demand. Exports, which comprised the bulk of the share, accounted for 23.06 percent of the total aggregate demand. Besides that, demands were driven more by intermediate consumption, final consumption and less by

Table 4.1 Composition of Demand by Sector at Market Prices

RM million	Intermediate consumption	Private consumption	Public consumption	Public investment	Private investment	Exports
Agriculture	66,898.73	47,729.75	2,039.64	1,442.05	6,180.2	9,340.81
Mining & quarrying	70,486.96	0.00	0	3,447.99	5,548.98	51,688.82
Industry	548,860.95	170,923.01	0	838	26,124.84	433,837.43
Electricity, gas & water	46,365.58	18,301.55	0	0	0	4.04
Building and constructions	35,304.65	0.00	30	91	134,588.93	4,077.97
Wholesale and retail trade	154,415.69	47,769.49	0	1,387.19	12,857.89	84,775.43
Hotel & restaurant	16,988.33	62,887.33	0	0	0	0
Transport	37,032.59	5,047.04	0	1,628.01	1,139.01	20,793.15
Communication	60,037.78	68,103.11	0	0	15,185.03	19,934.03
Financial, real estate & business	147,594.17	54,518.03	0	0	2,733	12,372.03
Business services	13,452.45	8,240.14	0	0	0	0
Education	2,103.168	27,372.70	34,189.87	3,395.09	0	0
Health	8,458.3	22,169.54	15,346.37	1,093.03	0	0
Recreation	1,232.41	18,472.56	0	0	0	1,506.96

RM million	Intermediate consumption	Private consumption	Public consumption	Public investment	Private investment	Exports
Other private services	3,242.92	5,135.75	0	0	0	0
Public administration	8,752.261	0.00	40,694.75	4,147.21	1,738.06	503.33
Public order and defense	0	0.00	26,745.96	5,085.37	0	0
Other public administration	0	0.00	4,712.41	696.06	0	0
Total	1,221,226.94	556,670	123,759	23,251	206,095.94	638,834
Pct of total	44.09	20.10	4.47	0.84	7.44	23.06

Source: Derived from Table 3.2.

investment. Intermediate consumption accounted for 44.09 percent of the total aggregate demand. Final consumption stood for 24.57 percent for both the public and private sectors compared to investment of 8.31 percent. The public sector share of the total final demand was 5.31 percent, of which 4.47 percent was due to public consumption and 0.84 percent was due to public investment. By all standards, this share was extremely low especially given the scope and size of the public sector production. In contrast, most of the demands for goods and services were from the private sector, which accounted for 27.54 percent of the total aggregate demands where 20.10 percent was due to private consumption and 7.44 percent to private investment.

Table 4.2 indicates that most intermediate consumption, final consumption and exports accrued to the industry sector, recorded 44.94 percent, 25.12 percent, 11.76 percent and 67.91 percent of their total, respectively. For the intermediate consumption, after industry, the consumption then accrued to the wholesale and retail trade, financial, real estate and business, mining and quarrying, agriculture and communications. For the final consumption, after industry, the consumption accrued to communications, hotel and restaurant, education, financial, real estate and business, and wholesale and retail trade. The final consumption in these five sectors accounted for 43.33 percent of the total final consumption.

While for the investments, most of the investments were made in building and constructions with a record of 58.72 percent, followed by industry, communications, wholesale and retail trade, mining and quarrying, and agriculture with a record 31.83 percent of the total investments. On the other hand, exports for the other sectors, other than industry, were very low. Most of the exports for the other sectors were less than 2 percent of the total exports except for exports in the wholesale and retail trade (13.27 percent), mining

Table 4.2 Composition of Demand by Sector

	Intermediate consumption (RM million)	% of total	Final consumption (RM million)	% of total	Investment (RM million)	% of total	Exports (RM million)	% of total
Agriculture	66,898.73	5.48	49,769.39	7.31	7,622.25	3.32	9,340.81	1.46
Mining & quarrying	70,486.96	5.77	0	0	8,996.97	3.92	51,688.82	8.09
Industry	548860.95	44.94	170923.01	25.12	26962.84	11.76	433837.43	67.91
Electricity, gas & water	46,365.58	3.80	18,301.55	2.69	0	0	4.04	0
Building and constructions	35,304.65	2.89	30.00	0.00	134,679.93	58.72	4,077.97	0.64
Wholesale and retail trade	154,415.69	12.64	47,769.49	7.02	14,245.08	6.21	84,775.43	13.27
Hotel & restaurant	16,988.33	1.39	62,887.33	9.24	0	0	0	0
Transport	37,032.59	3.03	5,047.04	0.74	2,767.02	1.21	20,793.15	3.25
Communication	60,037.78	4.92	68,103.11	10.01	15,185.03	6.62	19,934.03	3.12
Financial, real estate & business	147,594.17	12.09	54,518.03	8.01	2,733	1.19	12,372.03	1.94
Business services	13,452.45	1.10	8,240.14	1.21	0	0	0	0
Education	2,103.168	0.17	61,562.57	9.05	3,395.09	1.48	0	0
Health	8,458.3	0.69	37,515.91	5.51	1,093.03	0.48	0	0
Recreation	1,232.41	0.10	18,472.56	2.71	0	0	1,506.96	0.24
Other private services	3,242.92	0.27	5,135.75	0.75	0	0	0	0
Public administration	8,752.261	0.72	40,694.75	5.98	5,885.27	2.57	503.33	0.08
Public order and defense	0	0	26,745.96	3.93	5,085.37	2.22	0	0
Other public administration	0	0	4,712.41	0.69	696.06	0.30	0	0
Total	1,221,226.94	100.00	680,429.00	100.00	229,346.94	100.00	638,834.00	100.00

Source: Derived from Table 3.2.

and quarrying (8.09 percent), transportation and communications (3.25 and 3.12 percent, respectively).

Overall, the sectoral demand revealed that the structure of demand in the Malaysian economy was largely supported by demand for the industrial sector, although the building and constructions sector had an exceptionally high investment. Therefore, it is inferred that the economic activities remained influenced significantly by the sectoral linkage effects because the highest sectoral demand was attributed to this sector rather than the other sectors.

The unequal distribution of resources also can be highlighted by the bias in the public and private sectoral composition of investments and consumption. The distribution of the resources for both the public and private sectors is not uniform across sectors. First, the book briefly highlights the unequal distribution of resources by the private sector and then a more detailed analysis of the unequal distribution of resources by the public sector is discussed in the following sections.

As indicated in Table 4.3, most of the capital goods that were used for private investments were from the building and constructions sector, which

Table 4.3 Composition of Private Sector Demand

	Private consumption (RM million)	Pct of total private consumption	Private investment (RM million)	Pct of total private investment
Agriculture	47,729.75	8.57	6,180.2	3.00
Mining & quarrying	0.00	0	5,548.98	2.69
Industry	170,923.01	30.70	26,124.84	12.68
Electricity, gas & water	18,301.55	3.29	0	0
Building and constructions	0.00	0	134,588.93	65.30
Wholesale and retail trade	47,769.49	8.58	12,857.89	6.24
Hotel & restaurant	62,887.33	11.30	0	0
Transport	5,047.04	0.91	1,139.01	0.55
Communication	68,103.11	12.23	15,185.03	7.37
Financial, real estate & business	54,518.03	9.79	2,733	1.33
Business services	8,240.14	1.48	0	0
Education	27,372.70	4.92	0	0
Health	22,169.54	3.98	0	0
Recreation	18,472.56	3.32	0	0
Other private services	5,135.75	0.92	0	0
Public administration	0.00	0	1,738.06	0.84
Public order and defense	0.00	0	0	0
Other public administration	0.00	0	0	0
Total	556,670	100.00	206,095.94	100.00

Source: Derived from Table 3.2.

accounted for 65.30 percent of the total private investments. It was followed by the industry (12.68 percent), communications (7.37 percent), and the wholesale and retail trade (6.24 percent). Similarly, most of the private consumption accrued to the industry sector recorded 30.70 percent of the total private consumption but it was followed by the consumption on communications (12.23 percent), hotel and restaurant (11.30 percent), financial, real estate and business (9.79 percent), and agriculture (8.57 percent).

The high rate of private investment and consumption in certain sectors put the sectors in a vulnerable position facing disinvestments and rapid depreciation of their capital stock. Most vulnerable of all were the financial, insurance and real estate sectors, which had extremely high consumption shares but relatively low exports and no public investment. Meanwhile, the low level of private consumption (8.57 percent) and private investment (3.0 percent) on the agricultural and livestock sector amplified the difficulties of this sector.

4.2.2   Public Sector Allocation of Resources

This section reviews the initial pattern of the public sector expenditure, which prevailed in the base year 2015. From Table SAM (Table 3.2), across the row of the current account of the public sector (row 44), there were income taxes from the households, corporate taxes, dividends and royalties from the companies, indirect taxes, and domestic financing and financing from ROW. Altogether the sum across row 44 provides the aggregate current account of the public sector or the total resources accrued to the public current accounts during 2015. These resources were RM179,304 million representing only 15.23 percent of the GDP (RM1,176,941 million). Taxes (direct and indirect) accounted for well above 80 percent of the total, of which direct taxes represented 50.19 percent and indirect taxes 29.93 percent.

The columns for the public sector current account (column 44) of Table SAM show the current expenditure for public consumption, public transfer to households, public savings and payment to the ROW. Out of the public current expenditure, public consumption in the production sectors formed the largest proportion (69.02 percent), followed by public saving (19.61 percent), current transfer to households (10.53 percent) and payment to ROW (0.85 percent). The high proportion of public consumption in the production sectors could reflect the importance of the different programs of the public sector purchasing policies in income distribution. In addition, high public current transfer to household could directly reflect the government's commitments toward poverty reduction and income equality. On the other hand, low spending on transaction with the ROW (RM1,518 million) could reflect the low and sustainable level of the external debt.

Table 4.4 Share in Public Current Expenditure

	RM million	*% of total*
Public consumption in production sectors	123,759	69.02
Current transfer to households	18,872	10.53
Payment to ROW	1,518	0.85
Savings (current surplus)	35,155	19.61
Total	179,304	100.00

Source: Derived from Table 3.2.

Table 4.5 Share in Public Consumption in Production Sectors

Sector	*RM million*	*% of total*
Agriculture	2,039.64	1.65
Education	34,189.87	27.63
Health	15,346.37	12.40
Public administration	40,694.75	32.88
Public order and defense	26,745.96	21.61
Other public administration	4,742.41	3.83
Total	123,759.00	100.00

Source: Derived from Table 3.2.

Among the public consumption in the production sectors, public consumption on general administration formed the largest component (32.88 percent) followed by consumption on education (27.63 percent) and public order and defense (21.61 percent). Public consumption on the agricultural sector only accounted for 1.65 percent of the total aggregate of the public consumption.

The row of the capital account of the public sector (row 45) of the Table SAM records the savings of the public sector (RM35, 155 million) and the capital received from ROW (RM21,477 million). Altogether, the sum across row 45 provides the aggregated capital account of the public sector. These capitals are RM56,632 million representing only 4.81 percent of the GDP. The columns of the public sector capital account (column 45) record the capital expenditure such as public investments in the production sectors, indirect taxes and imported capital. Out of the public capital expenditure, public investments in the imported capital of RM32,625 million form the largest proportion (57.61 percent), followed by public investments in the production sectors (41.06 percent) and indirect taxes (1.33 percent).

Table 4.6 Share in Public Capital Expenditure

	RM million	% of total
Public investments in production sectors	23,251.00	41.06
Indirect taxes	756.00	1.33
Imported capital	32,625.00	57.61
Total	56,632.00	100.00

Source: Derived from Table 3.2.

Table 4.7 Share in Public Investment in Production Sectors

Sector	RM million	% of total
Agriculture & rural development	1,442.05	6.20
Industry	838.00	3.60
Trade	1,387.19	5.97
Transportation & communication	1,628.01	7.00
Education & health	4,488.12	19.30
General administration	9,232.58	39.71
Other public administration	4,235.05	18.21
Total	23,251.00	100.00

Source: Derived from Table 3.2.

Public investments in the production sectors were directed primarily to general administration (39.71 percent), education and health (19.30 percent), and other public administration (18.21 percent) as shown in Table 5.7. Altogether the public investment in these three sectors accounted for more than 75 percent of the total investment. The public investment in agriculture and rural development was low at 6.20 percent of the total investment, while industry had an extremely low public investment with only 3.60 percent.

The bias on composition in the sectoral demand, and more importantly, the bias on the public and private current and capital expenditure allocations might explain the continuing urban–rural and ethnic income disparity in Malaysia. The low level of consumption and capital formation, particularly in the agricultural sector, was a serious constraint to income inequality reduction.

4.2.3   *Household Income Distribution*

The distribution of household income among household groups, which prevailed in the base year 2015, was determined by three distributional mechanisms, namely, (a) the structure of production activities, (b) distribution of value-added from production to factors and (c) distribution of institutional

Table 4.8 Household Sources of Income

Sources	Value (RM million)	Pct
Labor income	412,240.14	68.04
Compensation of employee	250,690.30	
Mixed income*	161,549.84	
Dividend and social transfer from companies	174,754.09	28.84
Transfer from government	18,872	3.11
Total	605,866.23	100.00

Source: Derived from Table 3.2.

Note: * The operating surplus for household measures the surplus or deficit accruing from production before taking account of any interest, rent or similar charges payable on financial or tangible non-produced assets borrowed or rented by the unincorporated enterprise, or any interest, rent or similar receipts receivable on financial or tangible non-produced assets owned by the unincorporated enterprise.

income. The discussion on the distribution of income among the ethnic groups across regions will be about these three mechanisms.

Table 4.8, which is extracted from Table SAM, shows that 68.04 percent of the total household income was mainly derived from the production activities through the factor market (compensation of employee and household operating surplus), while the secondary sources of income such as distributed profits and transfer from companies, and transfer from government were recorded at only 28.84 percent and 3.11 percent, respectively. This indicated that the primary income distribution was the most important determinant of household income.

Production requires labor and capital as the input in the production process to produce an output. By supplying input to the production activities, labor receives the income in the form of compensation for the employees while the capital receives the operating surplus. Rows 19 to 28 in Table SAM (Table 3.2) show the income received by various categories of households (which own the labors) and the return of capitals from the production activities. They show that the total factorial income received from the domestic production was RM1,119,618.36 million, consisting of RM412,240.14 million or 36.82 percent from the labor factor and RM707,378.22 million or 63.18 percent from the capital.

The total factorial income received from the production activities or familiarly called value added generated by the production sectors is shown in Table 4.9. The industry sector formed the highest contributor to value added recorded at 21.87 percent of the total value added, followed by the wholesale and retail trade (15.94 percent), and financial, insurance and real estate (12.56 percent). On the other hand, agriculture-related activities, public sector-related activities, hotel and restaurant, health, education,

Table 4.9 Production Sectors Value Added: Percentage of Total Value Added

Sectors	Total (RM million)	Pct of total value added
Agriculture	97,379.05	8.70
Mining & quarrying	102,061.05	9.12
Industry	244,878.55	21.87
Electricity, gas & water	31,327.84	2.80
Building and constructions	52,143.04	4.66
Wholesale and retail trade	178,512.58	15.94
Hotel & restaurant	33,741.35	3.01
Transport	21,499.38	1.92
Communication	79,272.5	7.08
Financial, real estate & business	140,595.63	12.56
Business services	8,189.78	0.73
Education	44,544.79	3.98
Health	20,259.04	1.81
Recreation	8,943.34	0.80
Other private services	4,673.36	0.42
Public administration	34,407.04	3.07
Public order and defense	13,394.86	1.20
Other public administration	3,795.18	0.34
Total	1,119,618.36	100.00

Source: Derived from Table 3.2.

electricity, gas and water, business services, and building and constructions were among the lowest contributors to the value added.

The income generated by the production sectors to household, however, depends on the structure of the production activities. Some production sectors that are more labor-intensive will generate more income to the household as compared to others that are capital intensive. Table 4.10 shows that public sector-related activities, education, health, and building and construction sectors are considered as highly labor-intensive sectors; thus, they have a high capacity in generating income to the household. Income generated by the public sector-related activities, education and health were over 30 percent of their total value added. Most of the production sectors, however, were considered highly capital intensive, particularly mining and quarrying, electricity, gas and water, agriculture, recreation, financial, real estate and business, communication, and wholesale and retail trade. For mining and quarrying, for instance, 92.35 percent of the total sectoral value-added payment was constituted by the return on capital (operating surplus). The industrial sector, as a major contributor to the GDP, only generated income to the household by 21.46 percent compared to the return on capital

Table 4.10 Distribution of Value Added from Production Activities to Households

Sector	Labor incomes	Pct	Operating surplus	Pct	Total value added	Pct
	RM million		RM million		RM million	
Agriculture	19,329.77	14.21	116,708.82	85.79	136,038.59	100.00
Mining & quarrying	9,218.54	7.65	111,279.59	92.35	120,498.13	100.00
Industry	92,029.03	21.46	336,907.58	78.54	428,936.61	100.00
Electricity, gas & water	4,956.82	12.02	36,284.66	87.98	41,241.48	100.00
Building and constructions	38,314.52	29.75	90,457.56	70.25	128,772.08	100.00
Wholesale and retail trade	52,894.34	18.61	231,406.92	81.39	284,301.26	100.00
Hotel & restaurant	14,786.2	23.35	48,527.55	76.65	63,313.75	100.00
Transport	9,508.43	23.47	31,007.81	76.53	40,516.24	100.00
Communication	23,005.77	18.36	102,278.27	81.64	125,284.04	100.00
Financial, real estate & business	39,206.18	17.90	179,801.81	82.10	219,007.99	100.00
Business services	4,172.48	25.23	12,362.26	74.77	16,534.74	100.00
Education	38,561.23	31.69	83,106.02	68.31	121,667.25	100.00
Health	15,307.76	30.09	35,566.8	69.91	50,874.56	100.00
Recreation	2,372.90	17.33	11,316.24	82.67	13,689.14	100.00
Other private services	2,208.60	24.30	6,881.96	75.70	9,090.56	100.00
Public administration	31,270.45	32.25	65,677.49	67.75	96,947.94	100.00
Public order and defense	11,605.69	31.70	25,000.55	68.30	36,606.24	100.00
Other public administration	3,491.43	32.39	7,286.61	67.61	10,778.04	100.00

Source: Derived from Table 3.2.

by 78.54 percent. This reflected that the capacity of the industry sectors to generate income to the household was high as they were quite high capital intensive.

The public sector-related production had a rather low value-added, ranging between 0.5 and 5 percent of the aggregate value-added but it is the highest income-generating sector. This might reflect the fact that the public sector value-added was essentially made up of wage and salary outlays. Strikingly, the public sector value-added from returns on capital was moderately high, around 68 percent of the production with the continuation of the involvement of the government in the production process and in the more capital-intensive industries over the years.

Table 4.11 Distribution of Income to Household

Household	Income per household	Pct
Rural Malay	20,627.68	8.04
Rural Chinese	24,802.38	9.66
Rural Indians	23,167.18	9.02
Rural others	43,949.11	17.12
Urban Malay	22,303.02	8.69
Urban Chinese	28,893.54	11.26
Urban Indians	26,370.44	10.27
Urban others	63,626.23	24.78
Non-citizen	2,968.90	1.16
Total	256,708.47	100.00

Source: Derived from Table 3.2.

It appears in Table 4.11 that the distribution of income among the ethnic groups across the region was not equally distributed. It shows that both in the rural and urban areas the other races were the dominant income earners, who constituted 17.12 percent and 24.78 percent of the total household income, respectively. In the rural areas, after the other races, the income earners were followed by the Chinese (9.66 percent), Indians (9.02 percent) and Malays (8.04 percent). In the urban areas, the income earners after the other races were the Chinese (11.26 percent), Indians (10.27 percent) and Malays (8.69 percent). More significantly, the distribution of income for both regions showed that the urban area generated higher incomes for all ethnic groups than in the rural area. This characteristic was normal as most of the productive and industrial sectors in Malaysia were centered in the urban areas.

4.3   The Impact of Public Expenditure Policies in Reducing the Inter-Ethnic and Rural–Urban Disparity

The model of the Malaysian economy grounded in the SAM estimation can be the basis for further quantitative policy analysis. In this section, the SAM multiplier analysis was applied to show the impact of the public expenditure policies in reducing the inter-ethnic and rural–urban disparities. In the previous part, the SAM matrix was analyzed to highlight the structural relationships between public expenditure, and production activities, and income distribution.

This section starts with the review of the direct impact of public expenditure by looking at the public sector average expenditure propensities as shown in Table 4.12. This is to provide the basic understanding of how

Table 4.12 Production Sectors Average Expenditure Propensities

		Agriculture	Mining & quarrying	Industry	Electricity, gas & water	Building and constructions	Wholesale and retail trade
		1	2	3	4	5	6
Agriculture	1	0.0283	0.0000	0.0468	0.0000	0.0000	0.0114
Mining & quarrying	2	0.0002	0.0770	0.0484	0.0052	0.0205	0.0000
Industry	3	0.1081	0.0428	0.2897	0.1380	0.3409	0.1362
Electricity, gas & water	4	0.0031	0.0019	0.0191	0.0642	0.0027	0.0210
Building and constructions	5	0.0011	0.0084	0.0007	0.0885	0.0371	0.0256
Wholesale and retail trade	6	0.0284	0.0246	0.0879	0.0409	0.0734	0.0332
Hotel & restaurant	7	0.0028	0.0020	0.0016	0.0003	0.0004	0.0000
Transportation	8	0.0047	0.0084	0.0154	0.0060	0.0281	0.0047
Communication	9	0.0013	0.0043	0.0037	0.0053	0.0077	0.0103
Financial, real estate & business	10	0.0187	0.0152	0.0278	0.0221	0.0457	0.0814
Business services	11	0.0006	0.0001	0.0024	0.0016	0.0027	0.0066
Education	12	0.0000	0.0000	0.0000	0.0000	0.0000	0.0000
Health	13	0.0000	0.0000	0.0000	0.0000	0.0000	0.0000
Recreation	14	0.0000	0.0000	0.0000	0.0000	0.0000	0.0000
Other private services	15	0.0000	0.0000	0.0000	0.0041	0.0012	0.0008
Public administration	16	0.0000	0.0000	0.0000	0.0000	0.0000	0.0000
Public order and defense	17	0.0000	0.0000	0.0000	0.0000	0.0000	0.0000
Other public administration	18	0.0000	0.0000	0.0000	0.0000	0.0000	0.0000
Total primary inputs		0.1974	0.1847	0.5434	0.3762	0.5603	0.3313

(Continued)

Table 4.12 (Continued)

		Hotel & restaurant	Transportation	Communication	Financial, real estate & business	Business services	Education
		7	8	9	10	11	12
Agriculture	1	0.0657	0.0000	0.0000	0.0000	0.0000	0.0000
Mining & quarrying	2	0.0000	0.0000	0.0000	0.0000	0.0000	0.0000
Industry	3	0.2281	0.2561	0.0840	0.0346	0.0711	0.0758
Electricity, gas & water	4	0.0218	0.0022	0.0086	0.0046	0.0062	0.0344
Building and constructions	5	0.0029	0.0013	0.0224	0.0231	0.0278	0.0093
Wholesale and retail trade	6	0.0676	0.0480	0.0183	0.0078	0.0141	0.0220
Hotel & restaurant	7	0.0360	0.0307	0.0132	0.0048	0.0347	0.0151
Transportation	8	0.0128	0.0142	0.0100	0.0094	0.0326	0.0075
Communication	9	0.0106	0.1107	0.2018	0.0096	0.0097	0.0150
Financial, real estate & business	10	0.0334	0.0594	0.0592	0.1861	0.2432	0.0462
Business services	11	0.0041	0.0234	0.0086	0.0048	0.1071	0.0020
Education	12	0.0000	0.0000	0.0000	0.0000	0.0000	0.0134
Health	13	0.0000	0.0000	0.0000	0.0000	0.0000	0.0000
Recreation	14	0.0009	0.0000	0.0000	0.0000	0.0000	0.0011
Other private services	15	0.0004	0.0037	0.0042	0.0011	0.0005	0.0017
Public administration	16	0.0000	0.0000	0.0000	0.0000	0.0000	0.0619
Public order and defense	17	0.0000	0.0000	0.0000	0.0000	0.0000	0.0000
Other public administration	18	0.0000	0.0000	0.0000	0.0000	0.0000	0.0000
Total primary inputs		0.4842	0.5498	0.4302	0.2860	0.5470	0.3055

(Continued)

Table 4.12 (Continued)

		Health	Recreation	Other private services	Public administration	Public order and defense	Other public administration
		13	14	15	16	17	18
Agriculture	1	0.0000	0.0000	0.0000	0.0000	0.0000	0.0000
Mining & quarrying	2	0.0000	0.0000	0.0000	0.0000	0.0000	0.0000
Industry	3	0.1443	0.0932	0.0401	0.0763	0.1134	0.0598
Electricity, gas & water	4	0.0418	0.0388	0.0099	0.0351	0.0190	0.0650
Building and constructions	5	0.0058	0.0091	0.0000	0.0341	0.0163	0.0061
Wholesale and retail trade	6	0.0315	0.0220	0.0119	0.0224	0.0229	0.0231
Hotel & restaurant	7	0.0177	0.0364	0.0017	0.0304	0.0364	0.0191
Transportation	8	0.0110	0.0031	0.0012	0.0480	0.0121	0.0126
Communication	9	0.0043	0.0565	0.1652	0.0195	0.0590	0.0212
Financial, real estate & business	10	0.0494	0.1745	0.0997	0.0623	0.0346	0.0277
Business services	11	0.0035	0.0238	0.0208	0.0033	0.0009	0.0282
Education	12	0.0009	0.0000	0.0000	0.0000	0.0365	0.0000
Health	13	0.1797	0.0000	0.0000	0.0000	0.0000	0.0000
Recreation	14	0.0162	0.0060	0.0000	0.0020	0.0009	0.0117
Other private services	15	0.0023	0.0028	0.0687	0.0036	0.0070	0.0004
Public administration	16	0.0061	0.0000	0.0000	0.0000	0.1354	0.0001
Public order and defense	17	0.0000	0.0000	0.0000	0.0000	0.0000	0.0000
Other public administration	18	0.0000	0.0000	0.0000	0.0000	0.0000	0.0000
Total primary inputs		0.5144	0.4662	0.4193	0.3370	0.4943	0.2750

changes in the public sector expenditure would have an impact on household income. In the production sectors, each RM1 of the public general administration output required RM0.076 of input from the industry, RM0.062 from financial, real estate and business, RM0.048 from transportation and RM0.337 from the total primary input. Each RM1 of the public order and defense output required RM0.135 of inputs from public general administration, RM0.113 from the industry, RM0.059 from communications and RM0.494 from the total primary input.

Meanwhile, RM1 of other public administration output required RM0.065 of input from electricity, gas and water, input to the value of RM0.060 from the industry, business services to the value of RM0.028 and the total primary input valued at RM0.275. Despite this, each RM1 of the agriculture and livestock output required RM0.028 of input from within its own sector, input to the value of RM0.108 from the industry, the wholesale and retail trade to the value of RM0.028, and the total primary input valued at RM0.197. Each RM1 of the industry output required RM0.290 from within its own sector, input to the value of RM0.088 from the wholesale and retail trade, mining and quarrying to the value of RM0.048, agriculture to the value of RM0.047 and the total primary input valued at RM0.543.

In the production sectors, it appears that the public sector activities had no direct inter-industry linkage with the agriculture and livestock activities but had strong linkages with the industry. In addition the public sector activities and the industry had strong linkages with primary inputs. In contrast, agriculture had low linkages with primary input.

The direct and indirect impacts of the public expenditure policies in reducing the inter-ethnic and the rural–urban disparities were analyzed by applying the SAM-based fixed-price multiplier analysis. This was done through the discussion on the impact of the public expenditure expansion on the distribution of income across different household groups during the Eleventh Malaysia Plan (Experiment 1).

Results in Table 4.13 show that the public expenditure expansion in the plan improved household incomes. The total household income grew significantly at 6.28 percent per annum in the Eleventh Malaysia Plan. At the end of the planning period (2020), RM982.46 billion of household income was created, larger than the amount of the income of RM681.90 billion, generated at the beginning of the plan (2015).

Disaggregating household into different categories of ethnic groups and regions as in Table 4.13 gives a clearer picture of the impact of the public expenditure expansion on income distribution across different household groups. The results show that in the Eleventh Malaysia Plan, the public expenditure expansion significantly improved the distribution of income across different household groups. The table shows that the improvement

Table 4.13 Effects of the Eleventh Malaysia Plan Public Sector Expenditure Expansion on Household Income Distribution

Households	RM million			Average annual growth rate (Pct)
	2015	Average annual expenditure during 11MP	2020	2015–2020
Malay	420,544.08	632,053.95	634,040.68	7.08
Chinese	185,603.63	245,289.33	246,839.04	4.87
Indian	50,897.25	69,794.85	70,754.54	5.64
Others	15,573.45	18,699.58	18,895.05	3.27
Rural households	**153,194.57**	**232,803.11**	**232,469.70**	**7.20**
Rural Malay	131,831.48	204,128.09	203,776.60	7.53
Rural Chinese	13,889.33	18,560.55	18,580.82	4.97
Rural Indian	3,034.90	4,634.12	4,606.94	7.20
Rural others	4,438.86	5,480.35	5,505.34	3.65
Urban households	**519,423.84**	**733,034.60**	**738,059.61**	**6.03**
Urban Malay	288,712.60	427,925.86	430,264.08	6.88
Urban Chinese	171,714.30	226,728.78	228,258.22	4.86
Urban Indian	47,862.35	65,160.73	66,147.60	5.54
Urban others	11,134.59	13,219.23	13,389.71	3.12
Non-citizen	9,280.79	11,722.84	11,934.33	4.28
Total income	**681,899.20**	**965,837.71**	**982,463.64**	**6.28**
Pct of total income				
Rural households	22.47	24.10	23.66	
Urban households	76.17	75.90	75.12	
Non-citizen	1.36	1.21	1.21	

in the aggregate income of the household between 2015 and 2020 was largely contributed by the increase in the income of the urban households. The impact on the income of the urban household was far higher than the impact on the income of the rural households for all ethnic groups. Though the urban household contributed significantly to the total household income, the book indicates that the growth rate estimates in both plans provided more opportunities to the rural households to increase their levels of income. The growth rate of income in the rural area was 7.20 percent per annum, which was slightly higher than that of the urban area at 6.03 percent per annum. The difference between the total incomes earned by the rural and the urban households, however, was still wide and persistent and thus the income inequality among the ethnic groups was still largely explained by the regional income inequality.

Even though incomes for all the ethnic groups improved due to the public expenditure expansion, the growth rates of incomes among them differed significantly. The Malays registered the highest growth rate of income, followed by the Indians, the Chinese and the other races. A similar pattern also appeared for both the rural and urban areas where the Malay income growth rate was the highest. In contrast, the growth rate of the other races' income registered the lowest in both the rural and urban areas.

In absolute terms, the result revealed that the Malays' incomes registered the highest impact in both the rural and urban areas than the other ethnic groups as a consequence of the public expenditure expansion. The highest income impact on the Malays in the rural areas, however, did not mean that each of the Malay household received the highest income among the households as this exercise (multiplier impact) captured the effect of the total income of the household groups by ignoring the number of households in that group in the economy. Therefore, the book extends the analysis by dividing the total household income for each ethnic group by the number of households of the respective groups. This would get the per capita or per household income received by each of the households. The number of households by ethnic and strata for year 2015 was obtained directly from the Malaysian Economy in Figures, 2017. Due to the unavailability of the time series data on the number of households by ethnic and strata from the year 2015 to 2020, the book generates the number of households for this period by assuming that the proportional population distribution of the study population was virtually the same across the years. The figure 6.28 percent is based on the national population forecasting for the year 2020 in the Eleventh Malaysia Plan. Table 4.14 shows the income per household that was derived from Table 5.13.

Then, the income per household figure was used to calculate the household income disparity ratio among the ethnic groups. Table 4.15 shows the household income disparity ratio, which could act as an indicator of the income inequality for the base year and during the Eleventh Malaysia Plan. Compared to the base year, the result indicates that income inequality among the ethnic groups improved as a result of the public expenditure expansion. For example, the income inequality between the Malays and the Chinese reduced from 1:1.28 in the base year to 1:1.15, while for the Malays and the Indians, it reduced from 1:1.17 to 1:1.10. Similarly, the income disparity between the rural and the urban areas improved. Income disparity between the rural and the urban areas improved from 1:1.17 in the base year to 1:1.08. Income inequality in the urban area was higher than in the rural area in the base year. Income inequality for the Malays and the Chinese, for example, in the urban area was 1:1.30 and 1:1.20 in the rural area. Due to

Table 4.14 Effects of the Eleventh Malaysia Plan Public Sector Expenditure Expansion on Income Distribution – Income per Household

Households	2015	Average annual expenditure during 11MP	2020
Malay	21,922.75	32,687.94	33,052.22
Chinese	28,041.04	37,719.41	37,292.50
Indian	25,628.02	35,865.80	35,626.66
Others	57,255.33	67,752.10	69,467.10
Rural households	**21,327.38**	**32,410.29**	**32,363.87**
Rural Malay	20,627.68	31,939.93	31,884.93
Rural Chinese	24,802.38	33,143.84	33,180.04
Rural Indian	23,167.18	35,374.96	35,167.48
Rural others	43,949.11	54,260.89	54,508.32
Urban households	**24,880.2**	**35,110.38**	**35,352.76**
Urban Malay	22,303.02	33,057.23	33,237.86
Urban Chinese	28,893.54	38,150.56	38,407.91
Urban Indian	26,370.44	35,901.23	36,444.96
Urban others	63,626.23	75,538.46	76,512.63
Non-citizen	2,968.90	3,750.11	3,817.76
Total income	**21,865.56**	**31,345.13**	**31,502.35**

Source: Derived from Table 4.13 after dividing the total income for each ethnic group by the number of households of its respective groups.

Table 4.15 Household Income Disparity Ratio as a Result of the Public Expenditure Expansion

Households	Base year (2015)	11MP
Malay: Chinese	1.28	1.15
Malay: Indian	1.17	1.10
Malay: Other	2.61	2.07
Rural		
Malay: Chinese	1.20	1.04
Malay: Indian	1.12	1.11
Malay: Other	2.13	1.70
Urban		
Malay: Chinese	1.30	1.15
Malay: Indian	1.18	1.09
Malay: Other	2.85	2.29
Rural: Urban	1.17	1.08

Source: Derived from Table 5.14.

the public expenditure expansion, income inequality in the rural as well as the urban areas improved; however, income inequality in the urban areas was still higher than in the rural areas.

This result reveals that the public expenditure expansion in the Eleventh Malaysia Plan gave more opportunities to the Malays to increase their incomes and therefore, the public expenditure expansion had a significant impact on reducing the Malay–Chinese income inequality, as well as the Malay–Indian and the Malay–others income inequality but at a lesser extent. The public expenditure expansion also reduced the regional urban-rural income inequality during this period.

Overall, the result reflects that the public expenditure expansion in the Eleventh Malaysia Plan has improved the household income inequality. Nevertheless, the result also indicates that the increase in the total public expenditure from the base year to the plan still did not promise the reduction of income inequality at the same magnitude.

The result above could indicate that despite the expansion of the public sector expenditure in the Eleventh Malaysia Plan, there was difference in the pattern of the components of the public sector expenditure in the plan that influenced income distribution among the household sector. Thus, it is very crucial to evaluate the impacts of the various components of the public expenditure in the household income distribution. The different effects of the public sector expenditure programs on the incomes of household groups can be verified by looking at the multipliers corresponding to the impact of the 12 public expenditure programs on the incomes of the ninth socio-economic groups as shown in Table 4.16. From the rows, one can readily determine which program would be the most or least beneficial to any given household group.

As indicated earlier, the 12 public expenditure programs were categorized into two major categories, six public current expenditures and six public capital investments. Generally, it appeared that the public current expenditure impact on household income was higher than the public capital investment. The difference, however, was relatively comparable if the total amount of public current expenditure of RM289.8 billion, which was almost seven times higher than the public capital investment of RM63.5 billion, was taken into account.

For both categories, the public current expenditure and the public capital investment, it can be seen that for all the ethnic groups, regardless of rural or urban areas, public expenditure on others had the greatest positive impact on incomes except for other races and non-citizens. An RM1 public expenditure on others increased the income of the various households as follows: the urban Malay by RM0.1065, the rural Malay by RM0.0610, the urban Chinese by RM0.0404, the urban Indian by RM0.0110, the rural Chinese

Table 4.16 Impact of Difference Public Expenditures Programs on Incomes of Socioeconomic groups

Households	GovExpAgri& RurDev	GovExp Edu	GovExp Health	GovExpGen Admin	GovExp Def&Sec	GovExp Others	GovInvAgri &RuralDev	GovInv Industry	GovInv Trade	GovInvTransp &Comm	GovInvEdu &Health	GovInvGen Admin
Rural Malay	0.0445	0.0501	0.0290	0.0594	0.0465	0.0610	0.0445	0.0195	0.0228	0.0208	0.0455	0.0594
Rural Chinese	0.0055	0.0028	0.0021	0.0032	0.0029	0.0039	0.0055	0.0026	0.0036	0.0027	0.0027	0.0032
Rural Indian	0.0010	0.0007	0.0004	0.0016	0.0015	0.0014	0.0010	0.0005	0.0005	0.0008	0.0006	0.0016
Rural Others	0.0013	0.0006	0.0006	0.0006	0.0008	0.0008	0.0013	0.0007	0.0009	0.0007	0.0006	0.0006
Urban Malay	0.0491	0.1146	0.0828	0.0912	0.0827	0.1065	0.0491	0.0477	0.0584	0.0603	0.1076	0.0912
Urban Chinese	0.0311	0.0384	0.0423	0.0372	0.0336	0.0404	0.0311	0.0326	0.0504	0.0342	0.0392	0.0372
Urban Indian	0.0064	0.0112	0.0155	0.0176	0.0156	0.0110	0.0064	0.0082	0.0080	0.0122	0.0122	0.0176
Urban Others	0.0016	0.0013	0.0016	0.0016	0.0030	0.0012	0.0016	0.0011	0.0016	0.0012	0.0014	0.0016
Non-citizens	0.0036	0.0016	0.0020	0.0012	0.0035	0.0013	0.0036	0.0017	0.0014	0.0013	0.0017	0.0012
Total	0.1441	0.2213	0.1762	0.2136	0.1901	0.2275	0.1441	0.1146	0.1475	0.1343	0.2115	0.2136

Source: Derived from Table 4.4

Notes: Refer to Appendix 1 to get the full form of public current expenditure and public investment programs.

by RM0.0039 and the rural Indian by RM0.0014. This meant that it had given more impact to the urban Malay compared to the urban Chinese and the urban Indian but it was a smaller impact to the rural Indian compared to the rural Malay and the rural Chinese.

Public current expenditure on education had a very significant impact in increasing the income of the households. In fact, for the urban Malay households, current expenditure on education had the greatest impact on their incomes. For the rural Malay, the rural Chinese and the urban others, the public current expenditure in education had the second greatest impact on their incomes after the other public expenditure. The impact of the public current expenditure in education on the urban Malay, the urban Chinese and the urban Indian was significantly greater than the rural Malay, the rural Chinese and the rural Indian. For the rural Malay, the impact was two times less than the urban Malay. An RM1 public current expenditure in education increased the income of the urban Malay household by RM0.1146, the rural Malay household by RM0.0501, the urban Chinese household by RM0.0384 and the urban Indian household by RM0.0112. For the rural Chinese and the rural Indian, the public current expenditure in education had the third greatest impact on their incomes. In total, an RM1 increase in the public current expenditure on education increased the income of the households by RM0.2213. Meanwhile, the public investment in education and health also had a very significant impact in increasing the incomes, particularly for the urban Malay households.

Public current expenditure in general administration and public investment in general administration were also favorable programs not only for the urban households but also for the rural households for all groups. Meanwhile, public investment in the industry and in transportation and communication was among the lowest multiplier impacts of increasing household income. But still, these two types of the public expenditures were mostly benefited the urban areas. The Malay income was the most compared to other household groups. Surprisingly, for public investment in transportation and communication, although it accounted for the highest proportion of the total development expenditure as indicated in Chapter 2, it recorded the second lowest impact on increasing household incomes. Similarly, for public investment in the industry, although the industrial sector accounted for the highest sectoral demand and showed strong linkages with public sector activities as indicated in Sections 5.2.1 and 5.3, it recorded the lowest impact on increasing household incomes. Nevertheless, Section 5.3 has already shown that the industrial sector had a low direct impact on primary input.

Public investment in agriculture and rural development also had a low impact on the household income but the impact was higher than the public investment in the industry, as well as in transportation and communication.

The total multiplier effect was at 0.1441 but this result could be due to the very low expenditure allocated for this component (the current expenditure in education was more than ten times higher than the investment in agriculture and rural area development). Surprisingly, the impact of investment in agriculture and rural development on the rural household incomes was lower than the urban household incomes for all the ethnic groups. Indeed, public investment in agriculture and rural development should be able to generate more incomes for the rural households who were mainly involved in agricultural activities. This investment, nevertheless, benefitted more Malay households than other ethnic households in the rural as well as urban areas. The impact on the urban Malay was greater than the rural Malay, and the urban and rural Chinese.

All the public expenditure programs appeared to benefit the urban household groups significantly more than the rural household groups for all the ethnic groups. More obvious were the public current expenditure in education and health and public investment in education and health, which benefitted significantly more urban Malays than rural Malays and urban Chinese than rural Chinese; and the public investment in the wholesale and retail trade benefitted significantly more urban Malays than rural Malays and the urban Chinese. The public current expenditure in education, together with public investment in education and health, was relatively labor-intensive benefiting the urban household groups, most of the labor living in the urban areas.

The impact of the public expenditure programs also seems to favor the Malay household groups as opposed to the other ethnic groups in the rural or urban areas. Public current expenditure in education, public investment in education and health, public investment in agriculture and rural development, public current expenditure in general administration, public investment in general administration and public current expenditure on others have greater positive impacts on their relative positions in the income distribution. However, a few important specific programs such as the public investment in industry, public investment in the wholesale and retail trade, and public investment in transportation and communication marginally generated more incomes for the Malay household compared to the other ethnic groups.

This result reflects the pattern or public expenditure allocation in various public expenditure programs that had important implications on inter-ethnic and rural–urban disparities.

To further evaluate the impacts of the different components of the public expenditure in income distribution, a comparison between Experiment 1 and Experiment 2 was made. This helped to answer the question of what the likely impacts of the two alternative counterfactual public expenditure expansion scenarios (selective or equiproportional) would have been as these alternatives had been adopted at the outset of the Eleventh Malaysia Plan. These counterfactual experiments could show the importance of the selective programs of the public sector expenditure to achieve income equality goals.

Experiment 1 entailed the selective proportional expansion as occurred in the Eleventh Malaysia Plan compared to the base year 2015 where each individual category of the public expenditure in 2015 rose in proportion to the increase in each individual category in the actual Eleventh Malaysia Plan for the base year 2015. On the other hand, Experiment 2 entailed an equal proportional growth in each individual program of the current expenditure of 33.6 percent and a capital investment of 55.8 percent. The figure 33.6 percent was based on the total public current expenditure growth during the Eleventh Malaysia Plan for the base year 2015, and 55.8 percent on the total public capital investment growth during the national plan for the base year 2000. Table 4.17 shows an exogenous public expenditure created for these two experiments.

Looking at the impact on income distribution by the socioeconomic groups of Experiments 1 and 2 compared to the base year, as shown in Table 4.18, a few observations could be suggested. Under selective public

Table 4.17 Comparison of Experiments 1 and 2: Exogenous – Public Expenditure

Public expenditure	Base year 2015	Selective public expenditure growth (Experiment 1)		Selective public expenditure growth (Experiment 2)	
	RM million	Growth (Pct)	RM million	Growth (Pct)	RM million
PubCExpAgri&RurDev	2,039.64	17.69	5,420.69	20.93	6,379.49
PubCExpEducation	34,189.87	12.46	69,177.52	12.56	69,524.79
PubCExpHealth	15,346.37	12.15	30,539.27	11.37	29,279.50
PubCExpAdmin	40,694.75	−11.50	19,548.67	−9.53	22,318.88
PubCExpOrder&Defense	26,745.96	3.42	32,726.77	5.22	36,302.60
PubCExpOthers	4,742.41	67.17	103,495.71	64.15	92,789.20
PubInvAgri&RurDev	1,442.05	15.98	3,509.65	22.35	4,837.59
PubInvIndustry	838.00	21.54	2,701.29	25.72	3,308.03
PubInvTrade	1,387.19	21.54	4,471.59	25.72	5,475.97
PubInvTransp&Com	1,628.01	43.44	14,179.61	36.28	10,429.25
PubInvEduc&health	4,488.12	14.83	10,291.49	13.63	9,659.60
PubInvAdmin	9,232.58	−16.98	3,023.83	−19.88	2,442.94

Source: Derived from Table 4.4 and **11MP**.

Note: Refer to Appendix 1 to get the full form of public current expenditure and public investment programs.

Table 4.18 Comparison of Experiments 1 and 2: Household Incomes Distribution

	RM million			Index		
	Base year 2015	Selective PubExp growth Experiment 1	Equiproportional PubExp growth Experiment 2	Base year 2015	Selective PubExp growth	Equiproportional PubExp
PubCExpAgri&RurDev	2,039.64	5,420.69	6,379.49	100.00	265.77	312.78
PubCExpEducation	34,189.87	69,177.52	69,524.79	100.00	202.33	203.35
PubCExpHealth	15,346.37	30,539.27	29,279.50	100.00	199.00	190.79
PubCExpAdmin	40,694.75	19,548.67	22,318.88	100.00	48.04	54.84
PubCExp Order&Defense	26,745.96	32,726.77	36,302.60	100.00	122.36	135.73
PubCExpOthers	4,742.41	103,495.71	92,789.20	100.00	2,182.34	1956.58
PubInvAgri&RurDev	1,442.05	3,509.65	4,837.59	100.00	243.38	335.47
PubInvIndustry	838.00	2,701.29	3,308.03	100.00	322.35	394.75
PubInvTrade	1,387.19	4,471.59	5,475.97	100.00	322.35	394.75
PubInvTransp&Com	1,628.01	14,179.61	10,429.25	100.00	870.98	640.61
PubInvEduc&health	4,488.12	10,291.49	9,659.60	100.00	229.31	215.23
PubInvAdmin	9,232.58	3,023.83	2,442.94	100.00	32.75	26.46
Malay	420,544.08	634,040.68	629,022.06	100.00	150.77	149.57
Chinese	185,603.63	246,839.04	245,660.09	100.00	132.99	132.36
Indian	50,897.25	70,754.54	70,468.63	100.00	139.01	138.45
Others	15,573.45	18,895.05	18,891.80	100.00	121.33	121.31

(Continued)

Table 4.18 (Continued)

	RM million			Index		
	Base year 2015	Selective PubExp growth Experiment 1	Equiproportional PubExp growth Experiment 2	Base year 2015	Selective PubExp growth	Equiproportional PubExp
Rural households	**153,194.57**	**232,469.70**	**230,750.37**	100.00	151.75	150.63
Rural-Malay	131,831.48	203,776.60	202,190.83	100.00	154.57	153.37
Rural-Chinese	13,889.33	18,580.82	18,495.49	100.00	133.78	133.16
Rural-Indian	3,034.90	4,606.94	4,572.24	100.00	151.80	150.66
Rural-Others	4,438.86	5,505.34	5,491.82	100.00	124.03	123.72
Urban households	**519,423.84**	**738,059.61**	**733,292.20**	100.00	142.09	141.17
Urban-Malay	288,712.60	430,264.08	426,831.23	100.00	149.03	147.84
Urban-Chinese	171,714.30	228,258.22	227,164.60	100.00	132.93	132.29
Urban-Indian	47,862.35	66,147.60	65,896.39	100.00	138.20	137.68
Urban-Others	11,134.59	13,389.71	13,399.98	100.00	120.25	120.35
Non-citizen	9,280.79	11,934.33	11,961.35	100.00	128.59	128.88
Total income	**681,899.20**	**982,463.64**	**976,003.93**	**100.00**	144.08	143.13
Pct of total income						
Rural households	22.47	23.66				
Urban households	76.17	75.12				
Non-citizen	1.36	1.21				

Source: Derived from Table 3.2.

Notes: Refer to Appendix 1 to get the full form of public current expenditure and public investment programs.

expenditure expansion in Experiment 1, the increase in incomes would have been higher for all socioeconomic groups than under the equiproportional public expenditure expansion. In particular, the pattern of the public sector expenditure in Experiment 1 provided greater protection to the urban Malays, rural Malays, urban Indians and rural Indians.

Probably the major reason why the urban Malay groups fared better in Experiment 1 was that the public investment in transportation and communication and public investment in education and health had increased a lot in Experiment 1 where the investments focused more on the urban Malay groups. On the other hand, the major reason why the rural household groups fared better in Experiment 1 was that the public investment in general administration had increased a lot in this experiment. The incident illustrates the changing economic base of the rural economy that the majority of rural household groups in earlier days obtained income mainly from the agricultural activities in the rural areas.

The results of these counterfactual experiments indicate the importance of selective programs of the public sector expenditure to achieve income equality goals.

4.4   Conclusion

This chapter elaborates mainly the constructed SAM of the base year 2015 with respect to the public and the private sectoral composition of investments and consumption. The income disparities among the ethnic groups across regions were also reviewed from the perspectives of (a) the structure of production activities; (b) distribution of value-added from production to factors and (c) distribution of incomes for institutions.

On the basis of the constructed SAM, the industrial economic activities contributed greatly to the demand structure of the nation's economy with high sectoral linkage effects, although massive investments were directed to the building and constructions sector. Explicitly, the asymmetric distribution of resources for both the public and private sectors would assimilate the continuing urban–rural and ethnic income disparity in Malaysia. On one side, more than half of the private investments had gone to the building and constructions sector, while the majority of the private consumption was directed to the industries. On the other side, a substantial portion of the public current expenditure was in the production sectors, in particular the general administration sector. Public investment in the capitals that were imported stood at the highest where there was a high allocation of the public investments in the production sectors of general administration, education and health, and other public administration. On top of that, the majority of the production sectors were considered highly capital intensive where they were less likely to generate more incomes to households compared to others that used labor-intensive. Besides, the distribution of income among the ethnic groups across the region was not equal where the other races were the dominant income earners on the basis of the period observed. The urban area generated strikingly high incomes for all ethnic groups than in the rural area due to the centrality of the productive and industrial sectors in the urban areas.

Policy experiments were conducted to capture what the implications of the public expenditure expansion programs would be for the inter-ethnic and the rural-urban disparity. Looking at the public sector average expenditure propensities, the public sector activities had no direct inter-industry linkage with the agriculture and livestock activities but had strong linkages with the industry linking to primary input. On the basis of the SAM-based fixed-price multiplier analysis, the public expenditure expansion programs in the Eleventh Malaysia Plan had a wonderful boost for social well-being. By taking the direct and indirect impacts into consideration, the distribution of income across different household groups was enhanced significantly as the increase in the income of the urban households was the main contributor. The Malay's income registered the highest impact in both the rural and urban areas compared to the other ethnic groups in absolute terms. To date, the rural–urban income gap reduced from 1:1.17 in the base year to 1:1.08. Besides, the income inequality between the Malays and the Chinese reduced from 1: 1.28 in the base year to 1:1.15 while in the case of the Malays and the Indians, it reduced from 1:1.17 to 1:1.10. Despite this, the empirical findings showed that the expansion of public expenditure that focused mainly on agriculture and rural development, education, health and general administration had impressive positive impacts on income distribution. The counterfactual experiments captured the public sector expenditure programs that had important implications for achieving income equality goals. It was discovered that the public investment in general administration was likely to have a profound impact on rural households. It depicted the changing economic base of the rural economy that was previously considered agriculture-dependent. It is interesting to note that the public investment in transportation and communication was likely to be supported by the urban Malay.

References

Malaysia, Department of Statistics. (2010). *Malaysia input-output tables, 2010*. Putra-jaya: DOSM.

Malaysia, Department of Statistics. (2014). *Malaysia economic statistics-time series*. Putra-jaya: DOSM.

Malaysia, Economic Planning Unit. (2010). *The eleventh Malaysia plan 2016–2020*. Kuala Lumpur: Percetakan Nasional Berhad.

5 Implications for Policy in Public Expenditure

5.1 Introduction

Malaysia's experience has shown that since 1970 Malaysia has achieved remarkable growth and development. The structure of the economy has been transformed from dependence on agriculture to a more broad-based economy. More importantly, remarkable success has been made in poverty eradication. However, the income distribution policy's successes were only in the initial years and for more than 30 years there was only a slight improvement in income inequality.

The income distribution maps closely follow Malaysia's pattern of development. This, in turn, is closely linked to ethnic settlement patterns and industrial structures. Historically, the Malays, the Chinese and the Indians were separated both geographically and occupationally. The Malay community lived in settlements along the coasts and riverbanks. They engaged mainly in rice cultivation, fishing and rubber tapping, far away from the growing urban economy. The Chinese were a more urban community, dominating trade and commerce, and trade in tin mining and commercial agriculture. While some Indians settled in towns, most were mainly concentrated in rubber estates and plantations.

Not unexpectedly, given the above, in 1970, poverty was markedly higher among the Malays than other communities. In 1970, approximately two-thirds of the Malay households were living below the poverty line. Poverty rates among the Chinese and the Indian households were 27.5 percent and 40.2 percent, respectively. As a result of the policies adopted by Malaysia, there have been tremendous declines among each of the ethnic groups, such as by 2002 the poverty rates were 7.3 percent, 1.5 percent and 1.9 percent for the Malays, the Chinese and the Indians, respectively. Ethnic income differences generally narrowed over the 1970–2004 period. The Gini coefficient fell during this period, most notably for 20 years up to 1990. However, over the last decade, income differences have widened where the

DOI: 10.4324/9781003302506-5

Gini coefficient increased from 0.452 in 1999 to 0.462 in 2004. The mean income for the Chinese remained about two times higher than that of the Malays and the urban mean household income even increased to more than two times higher than that of the rural mean household income. After that point, income differences narrowed where the Gini coefficient was only 0.4 in 2016. Although the income for the Chinese decreased to about 1.5 times higher than the Malays, the urbanites still had incomes twice as high as the rural residents.

Income inequality has always been an important agenda in the government policy, reflected in its fiscal policy, particularly the public expenditure programs. The government's emphasis on income equality, however, was different in different eras of administration. During the NEP period, emphasis was given to income equality achievement where public expenditure was given more to agricultural and rural area development. After the NEP period, public expenditure was given more to social sector development, particularly in education and hence, public expenditure in agriculture and rural development dropped tremendously. Improving the education of the population has been a key strategy of the country's long-term plan to eradicate poverty and to achieve income equality, which may lead to ultimately high economic growth. Substantial expenditure in education significantly contributed to the economic growth, reduced poverty and improved inter-ethnic income inequality but it widened the rural–urban disparities, hence attributing to overall higher income inequality. The NEM was considered as a milestone achievement after the NEP, especially in the midst of a challenging world economic environment. Aiming to make Malaysia become a *market-led, well-governed*, regionally integrated, *entrepreneurial* and *innovative* country in the future, people in the bottom income group and the vulnerable categories like the Bumiputera in Sabah and Sarawak were given priority, regardless of ethnicity or location. The slow growth in the average income for them was seen particularly worrisome, in particular, for those in the rural areas. Practical skill enhancement became a central concern to increase their earning ability through education, training and skill upgrading. Therefore, the sustainability of the economy and the community would be achieved in the future.

How the government increases public spending has important policy implications in terms of whether the poor are benefited. Of particular interest is the relative position of the Malay households as well as the rural households in income distribution. To design pro-poor public expenditure programs, policymakers need to assess the distributional effects of the spending programs. A useful tool for this is the SAM. The use of the multisector SAM model focusing on the public sector resource allocation mechanisms as a framework for analyzing income distribution issues is able to show how the important public expenditure programs affect the distribution of income to individuals or socioeconomic groups. Therefore, this book incorporates the detailed public expenditure of various programs in the SAM framework; thus, it successfully improves the existing SAM framework in Malaysia.

The purpose of this book is to assess and evaluate the income distribution impact of the public sector expenditure totally and by various components. According to Keuning and Thorbecke (1989), organizing various categories of expenditure by activities represents an improvement over the prevailing literature on this subject, which emphasizes the importance of the sectorial composition of the public sector purchases but leaves the impression that these sectorial purchases are the direct subject of the government's choice. Sectorial choice appears to be an important and strategic variable whereby the public sector can affect various economic variables of the system. Different programs absorb different sectorial purchases and therefore exhibit differences in income generation.

To sum up, the book has shown income inequality from 1970 to the 2010s and discussed its impacts of the public expenditure policies in Malaysia in the SAM framework based on macro- and micro-data from HIS, HES, Quarterly Bulletin Bank Negara reports, Economic Reports, Treasury Statistics and other publications. The remaining chapter is devoted to the recapitulation of the major findings of the study. Hence, the implication of the public expenditure expansion on income distribution is discussed in Section 5.2. Some practicable policy implications are drawn out in Section 5.3, with some recommendations for future research arising from the limitations of this study. The concluding remarks are in Section 5.4.

5.2 Public Expenditure Impact on Income Distribution

Unequal distribution is shown in the composition of the sectoral demand where demands are driven more by exports, intermediate consumption, final consumption and less by investment. Most of the demand for goods and services are from the private sector, whereas the public sector share in the final demand is low. The sectoral demand indicates that the structure of demand in Malaysian economy is largely supported by the demand by the industry followed by transportation and communications, financial, insurance and real estate, and wholesale and retail trade.

Specifically, the public sector allocation of resources indicates the bias on the public current and capital expenditure to the education sectors, but low expenditure in agricultural and rural area development. Furthermore, the analysis shows that sectors considered as highly labor-intensive sectors (public sector-related activities, education and health) have a high capacity in generating income to the household. Nevertheless, many other sectors are highly capital intensive, particularly the industrial sector. The book then shows that the distribution of income among the ethnic groups across regions was not equally distributed in 2015. In both the rural and urban areas, the dominant income earners were the other races, while the Malays were still the lowest income earners. The urban areas generated higher incomes for all the ethnic groups than in the rural areas. The bias on composition in the sectoral demand as well as the bias in the public and private expenditure allocations may explain the continuing income inequality in Malaysia.

Public expenditure expansion does improve inter-ethnic income disparity and rural–urban disparity. The public expenditure expansions in the Eleventh Malaysia Plan generate more benefits to the low-income groups, particularly the Malays. The analysis also indicates that the continuous increase in the total public expenditure from the base year to the plan did not promise consistent magnitude improvement in income inequality. It could reflect that different components of the public expenditure in the plan would have different impacts on income distribution.

Various impacts of the different components of public expenditure on income inequality are evidenced by the analysis on the income multiplier value. Public administration expenditure seems to have the greatest positive impact on all ethnic groups. Public current expenditure and public investment in education have a significant positive impact in increasing the income of the urban Malays, the rural Malays, the urban Chinese and the urban Indians. The increase of public expenditure in education improves the relative position of the Malays compared to other ethnic groups. However, it negatively affects the relative position of the rural household compared to the urban household for all ethnic groups. The impact on the increase in the income of the urban Malay is more than double the increase in the income of the rural Malay.

The increase in the public investment in agriculture and rural development seems to have the potential to improve the relative position of the rural Malays compared to the urban Malays and the urban Chinese, as the impact on the increase in the income of the rural Malays is about the same – just slightly lower – as the increase in the income of the urban Malays and the urban Chinese. The much lower total multiplier effects of public investment in agriculture and rural development, compared to the public expenditure in education, are attributed much to a lower allocation for this expenditure (more than eight times less). Other public expenditures such as public investment in the wholesale and retail trade, industry, and transportation and communication have low multiplier impacts, and benefit more urban Malays. The result reflects that the components of public expenditure play a significant role to the inter-ethnic and rural–urban income disparities.

Therefore, the result suggests that the impact of the public expenditure programs to reduce income inequality depends not only on the amount of spending but also on its allocations.

5.3 Policy Implications

The book presents evidence on the importance of public expenditure in improving income inequality where the public expenditure has a positive impact on income equality. Nevertheless, the significant achievement in income equality is closely related to the right allocation of the public expenditure toward the poor, and therefore the components of the public expenditure play a very important role. Hence, this book reflects that the lower impact of public expenditure contributed to the widening of the overall income inequality during the 2000s was due to the public expenditure benefits that have been less redistributive toward the poor. It is rather obvious that public expenditure-related benefits for the agricultural working population were reduced significantly, while the Malays who were low-income people were mostly involved in agricultural activities. It also shows that allocating more expenditure to the low-income people through the highest proportion of public investment in agriculture and rural development during the 1970s (NEP) has a remarkable impact on improving income inequality. The book also reflects that although the public sector had invested heavily in education in the 2010s, and as a consequence had improved the inter-ethnic income inequality, it was unable to reduce rural–urban disparity. Nevertheless, the narrowness of the overall income disparities happened during the 2010s. This was the consequence of the revolutionary change in social welfare policies – focusing only on the income levels of the bottom 40 percent households and the vulnerable categories with particular needs like the Bumiputera in Sabah and Sarawak, the ethnic minorities and the *Orang Asli* communities in Peninsular Malaysia, regardless of the regions. Indeed, in 2009, 73 percent of the population with the income levels of the bottom 40 percent households was the Bumiputera. In other words, they were the core group and formed a necessary part of the public entitlement programs.

The pattern of public expenditure allocation for different programs reflects the government's seriousness in achieving income equality goals. The move from the NEP (1970–1990), and the NDP (1991–2000) to the National Vision policy (2001–2010) and then to the National Transformation Programme (October 2020–2018) as reflected by the public expenditure allocations is seen as less aggressive in terms of income equality. This is understandable as it is known that unlike the NEP no significant framework was set for achieving distributive targets in the NDP. While there was still emphasis on the strategy of growth with equity, the NDP relied on the private sector to be responsive and pro-active in attaining these objectives. The latest NTP took on the inclusive development approach to fully benefit the community from the wealth of the country. The 12 NKEAs sought the government's initiative to stimulate jobs, investments and GNI that were grounded on the public–private collaborations.

Generally, the result shows that public expenditure does improve income inequality in Malaysia. The level of improvement in income inequality, however, is much dependent on the composition of the expenditure to the various programs. During the period where allocation of the expenditure was allocated more to the poor, the improvement in income inequality was much higher than the period where the allocation was more to the non-poor. In the 2010s, the pattern in the component of public expenditure had a relatively significant impact on public expenditure in improving income inequality compared to the 2000s, the 1980s and the 1970s.

In the 2010s, the components of the public expenditure contained higher proportions in education, health and general administration but a lower proportion in agricultural and rural area development. The impact of these elements of public expenditure seems to favor the Malay household groups as opposed to the other ethnic groups, as well as the urban household groups as opposed to the rural household. Hence, it could be said that the respective fiscal consolidation would have a slight improvement in the rural–urban income inequality compared to the income inequality of the ethnic groups. Although there was only a slow progress in improving the rural–urban income inequality with the ratio of 2.11 in 2004 to 1.76 in 2016, the overall impact on income distribution was reduced remarkably from 0.462 in 2004 and 0.441 in 2009 to 0.399 in 2016. This indicates that the implementation of the strategy to achieve equality goals has to be carried out carefully by putting more emphasis to reduce the disparity between the rural and the urban areas.

The expenditure programs for education could be continued but the efforts to increase and target expenditure on education must be complemented. Substantial reorganization of the sector is needed to make the supply of services reach the poor. One aspect of social stratification in Malaysia is that not all groups have equal access to formal education. The rich has greater access than the poor. The urban population has greater access than the rural. There is thus a strong prima facie case for reducing the concentration of educational expenditure on high-cost urban colleges and universities but distributing the resources broadly among the entire population instead. This implies in particular a reallocation of the expenditure to the primary and secondary schools and particularly to schools located in the rural areas where most of the poor are located and where historically education has been severely neglected.

The way forward is to ensure that access to universal education continues to be available especially for the poor and those in remote and sparsely populated areas. Future public policies on education will need to be sensitive to the possibility of an increasing urban–rural digital divide. Other aspects of education that require monitoring as Malaysia advances into the twenty-first century concern the need to ensure curriculum relevance, the quality of education amidst the changing needs in the economy, and the important role of the private sector in education. Another important aspect is the government should continue to ensure that there is a balance in spending on physical capital and human capital. This is to avoid misallocation of resources, placing no excessive emphasis on school construction (public investment) and sufficient emphasis on teachers and school supplies (public current expenditure).

Besides that, the expenditure program for agricultural and rural area development should bear more fruit in the future. This expenditure program is evident in the increase of the urban and rural Malay household income. The incidence of poverty in Malaysia has always been predominantly rural and as the majority in the rural areas is Malays, it is critical that poverty redress and income improvement programs be implemented in this area. As such, high priority should consistently be placed on agricultural and rural area development. Evidence in this book shows that during the NEP, allocation for agriculture and rural development amounted to a significant proportion of the public expenditure. Such a proportion was targeted to reduce income inequality and undeniably it was successful. In addition, the analysis in the base year 2015 showed that the small proportion of the public expenditure in agriculture and rural development caused a small multiplier impact on household income, despite the public expenditure having given more benefits to the Malays than the other ethnic groups.

While expenditure in agriculture and rural development does improve the income of the Malay households, their efficacy in achieving redistribution of income must be improved as the book shows that the urban Malay household has benefited more than the rural Malay household, though slightly higher. The program should focus on increasing the productivity of the agricultural and rural sector by introducing better technology and methods as well as improving rural infrastructure. To increase the participation of the rural population in income-generating activities, the scope for credit facilities for rural industries need to be expanded. They should be encouraged to be involved in modern farming and non-farming or off-farm activities. A higher allocation expenditure should be given to support the new programs and to pursue the existing programs, which are still relevant such as the efficient use of land, technical and financial assistance to farmers, and planting in big-sized plantations. The development of rural non-agricultural activities like production in small- and medium-sized enterprises (SMEs), which are seen now as not being sufficient, need to be given more emphasis to decrease the disparity between the urban and rural areas.

In order to reallocate the public expenditure to agriculture and rural development, it requires the percentage of the budget earmarked for activities which do not contribute much to the income equality to be reduced to a minimum. This includes spending on the wholesale and retail trade, industry, transportation and communication, public order and defense and excessively large bureaucracies in public administration. The revenues thus saved could be used to raise the proportion of expenditure devoted to agricultural and rural area development activities, which benefit the largest number of poor people. On the other hand, the government could also reallocate the expenditure in education to agricultural and rural area development. Besides that, if the spending in the wholesale and retail trade, and industry is crucial to be increased in order to increase Bumiputera participation in businesses, it has to be carried out carefully as it could result in the worst income equality.

Public expenditure policies must try to balance the expenditure for agriculture and rural development, education and other expenditure, noting that merely focusing on education may lead to lesser effects on income inequality. The balanced expenditure is a warrant for all the population to have access to the public services. This is a necessary condition for sustainable income equality and poverty reduction. The government should also note that different emphasis on income inequality reflected by the public expenditure composition in different eras of administration has contributed much to the change in income inequality throughout the years. Hence, the government should direct more expenditure to improve income inequality.

A desire to develop a country where inequality between ethnic groups is significant raises the question of the way to achieve it. The interventionist policies that focus on reducing the inequality of the highly vulnerable groups, especially the income levels of the lowest 40 percent households and the disadvantaged segments with particular needs such as the Bumiputera in Sabah and Sarawak, the ethnic minorities and the *Orang Asli* communities in Peninsular Malaysia, appear to provide a solution so far to balance economic growth and social development, in particular, the Malays who make up about 73 percent of the lowest income group. It follows that what matters for this approach with regard to equality is the equality between groups rather than between individuals. However, more importantly, addressing the rural–urban disparity is seen crucial now as the way of reducing overall income inequality. It is believed that addressing rural–urban disparity could automatically address the inter-ethnic income disparity because of the disproportionate presence of the Malays in rural areas. Although regional development was mentioned as early as the 1970s, efforts to implement the plans have been rather slow and little success has been achieved.

Since Malaysia has made enormous progress in eliminating poverty, it suggests that a change of emphasis in the public expenditure policy may now be called for. This book has suggested a number of possible future directions. First, the efforts to increase and target expenditure on education must be reorganized in order to achieve income equality goals. Second, the public expenditure policy may need to be increasingly directed at improving income inequality, investment in agriculture and rural development. Third, public investment in industry, wholesale and retail trade, and transportation and communication to generate more Bumiputera participation in businesses has to be carried out carefully as it could lead to the worst income distribution. Fourth, addressing the rural–urban disparity is seen as being more crucial than the inter-ethnic disparity as the way of reducing overall income inequality.

In conclusion, the book has managed to achieve the stipulated objective. The important policy lesson, which can be derived from this book, is the influence of the overall strategies for public expenditure on the outcomes of income distribution. Therefore, if the public expenditure policy aims to achieve income equality goals, it could pattern the components of the public expenditure to gear toward achieving the goals. The book has left the option to the public expenditure policies. If the policy is to achieve continuous high economic growth, a high allocation in education should be pursued but if the policy is to achieve high economic growth with higher income equality, the reallocation to public investment in agriculture and rural development needs greater attention. The public expenditure policy could also opt to maintain the high allocation in education but at the same time should allocate higher and sufficient allocation for agriculture and rural development through the reallocation of public investment in transportation and communication, public investment in industry, and public investment in the wholesale and retail trade.

5.4 Limitations and Further Research

Some further extensions could be pursued on the methodological side. First of all, further efforts should be directed to improve the estimated SAM. Additional information could probably be included in the public expenditure programs for the agriculture and education sectors. In agriculture, for example, separate accounts for agricultural and non-agricultural rural activities could be incorporated and considered as strategic for rural developmental processes.

In addition, a valuable improvement of SAM could be realized with the inclusion of factorial incomes according to the level of education or type of occupation. The inclusion of factorial income could extend the multiplier impact analysis by deriving the whole network of paths through which different patterns of public expenditure influence directly and indirectly the variables and sectors of the Malaysian socioeconomic system as represented by SAM. In particular, by using the structural path analysis, various direct and indirect paths can be identified through which given public expenditure expansion policies ultimately influence the incomes of different socioeconomic groups.

The conventional approach of the SAM impact analysis of the public expenditure is to multiply the vector of changes by the Leontief inverse or a set of multipliers. If the initial perturbation is positive, so too will be the indirect impacts. This approach therefore typically does not consider the fact that the increased spending will require a tax increase or raise the deficit, both having typically negative ramifications for the rest of the economy, for example, government transfer payments to households being financed by a reduction of the funds available for some other activity in the economy, rather than being an autonomous creation of income and a new economic activity.

The critiques of applying SAM in income distribution analysis are quick to point out the inherent limitations of this technique including linearity, absence of constraints, and omission of factor and product-pricing considerations. Another approach is to use computable general equilibrium (CGE) models with special distributional features. CGE can be considered as a complementary tool for SAM analysis. CGE models are able to overcome the limitations of SAM but the determinants of results are not readily transparent and are thus often criticized for their 'black box' impression.

Reference

Keuning, S., & Thorbecke, E. (1989). *The impact of budget retrenchment on income distribution in Indonesia: A Social Accounting Matrix application* (Working Paper No. 3). Paris, France: OECD Development Centre.

Appendix 1

Full Form of Public Expenditure

Short form	Number	Refer to
GovExpAgri&RurDev	29	Public current expenditure on agriculture and rural development
GovExpEdu	30	Public current expenditure on education
GovExpHealth	31	Public current expenditure on health
GovExpGenAdmin	32	Public current expenditure on general administration
GovExpDef&Sec	33	Public current expenditure on public order, security and defense
GovExpOthers	34	Public current expenditure on other public administration
GovExpTransfer	35	Public current expenditure on transfers
GovInvAgric&RuralDev	36	Public investment in agriculture and rural development
GovInvIndustry	37	Public investment in industry
GovInvTrade	38	Public investment in wholesale and retail trade
GovInvTransp&Comm	39	Public investment in transportation and communication
GovInvEduc&Health	40	Public investment in education and health
GovInvGenAdmin	41	Public investment in general administration
GovInvOthers	42	Public investment in other public administration
ROW current	48	Rest of the world current
ROW capital	49	Rest of the world capital

Index

For Product Safety Concerns and Information please contact our EU
representative GPSR@taylorandfrancis.com
Taylor & Francis Verlag GmbH, Kaufingerstraße 24, 80331 München, Germany

www.ingramcontent.com/pod-product-compliance
Lightning Source LLC
Chambersburg PA
CBHW061328220326
41599CB00026B/5080

* 9 7 8 1 0 3 2 2 9 8 8 6 3 *